UNDERSTANDING THE
NEW BIRTH

GREGORY K. RIGGEN

DEDICATION

This book is dedicated to Apostolic young people everywhere. You are extremely important to the Kingdom of God – not just in the future, but today. May you grow to know and love this glorious truth in greater measure than ever before. In so doing, you will be well equipped to deal with the onslaught of compromise and false doctrine facing the church today.

CONTENTS

ACKNOWLEDGMENTS

I would like to express my sincere appreciation to everyone who helped make this book a reality. First, it was Bishop Gary Howard's encouragement that became the catalyst for me to write. Second, my wife has spent untold hours reading, re-reading, editing, and working alongside me throughout this process. She was, is, and will ever continue to be a God-send for me! Also, Brother Jared Hilton has gone above and beyond the call of duty in helping me with this effort. I also appreciate the others who served as proofreaders and editors: Pastor John Burgess, Captain D.J. Uribe, USAF (my son-in-law), Pastor Brandon Hilton (also my son-in-law), Brother and Sister Douglas Goff, and Brother Andrew Merriman and his daughter, Maddison. Their input has been invaluable. Finally, I want to thank Sister Jasmine Olmos for the cover design. To each and every one of you, words are not adequate to convey my deep gratitude. The words, "Thank You!" just do not seem sufficient. I just want each of you to know that I am truly thankful.

PREFACE
THE REASON FOR WRITING

The book you now hold in your hands is the second in a series I am calling, *Understanding Apostolic Doctrine*. This one is considerably longer than the first one (*Understanding the Godhead*), but for a couple of very good reasons.

To begin with, in the first book, I was dealing with only one subject. Here, although the overall theme is the new birth, that theme encompasses several subtopics. Furthermore, there are some preliminary chapters I have included which do not deal with the new birth directly. In my estimation, however, they are important to the subject at hand. Finally, the chapter on baptism alone is approximately the same length as the entire Godhead book!

This book is not just the result of having loved this doctrine for more than 45 years. It is also the result of more than six years of working with pastors on the continent of Africa who were sincere in their beliefs, but sincerely wrong.

When I first began conducting what I now call "Truth Conferences" in Africa, I began using a particular format which I felt God had given me. Through the years, it has proven to be productive and extremely successful.

As I prepared to write this book on the new birth, I felt it was important to approach the subject using the same format we use in Africa. Rather than just jumping into subjects like baptism and the Holy Ghost, I want to first establish some important principles with regard to proper Bible interpretation.

I see this as necessary when dealing with those who have not heretofore embraced this message. If I can approach these subjects "precept upon precept" and "line upon line" (Isaiah 28:10), the hearers become much more open to topics they might otherwise outright reject.

Although I am well aware that the majority of my readers will be people who already believe the things about which I have written, I want to present these truths in such a way that if someone who does NOT believe this doctrine DOES take the time to read it, they, too, may see the truth in what I have presented.

Furthermore, by including these preliminary chapters, I also hope to provide believers with the tools which can help them in reaching others. If they, too, will follow the method of presentation I am using, I believe they can see the same level of success God has allowed me to experience.

As I have already stated, this is the second of what I expect to be at least three volumes, each focused on helping the reader to gain a proper understanding of a particular aspect of the Apostolic message. It is my hope that subsequent volumes will come together quickly.

My intention and purpose for writing is to provide publications that almost anyone can easily understand. I believe there is a genuine need to present our message in a way that remains true to "the simplicity that is in Christ" (2 Corinthians 11:3). In fact, I believe there is a real need in our movement to produce writings which can convince doubters and strengthen believers regardless of their spiritual or educational level.

Throughout the pages of this book, therefore, I hope to

present the doctrine of the new birth in such a way that "the wayfaring men, though fools, shall not err therein" (Isaiah 35:8). While I desire to be thorough, I have no intention of delving into a deep theological exegesis. Rather, I want to let Scripture interpret Scripture and thereby offer answers for the "common man."

In case you have not read my first volume, I should perhaps take some time to provide a glimpse into my personal testimony. I was not born into an Apostolic home. While my parents considered themselves Christians, they were not "practicing" any particular religion. They instilled in us a belief in God, but that was about as far as it went. They did not teach us about the Bible, and they did not take us to church.

Through a series of events, God brought my family to a place of desperation. We went from having a comfortable income to extreme poverty in a matter of months. At the age of 11, a teenage cousin invited me to visit an Apostolic church. I went and loved it. We lived close enough that I could walk to church if necessary, and, shortly after turning 12, I was baptized in Jesus' name and filled with the Holy Ghost. That summer, I felt God's call to preach. Within a few months of my conversion, my parents, siblings, and grandmother were subsequently converted. About a year and a half after I prayed through, I preached my first sermon at the age of 13.

Not long after that, I was invited to attend a debate between an Apostolic preacher and a preacher from another denomination. I watched as the Apostolic preacher quoted Scriptures and defended the message, doing it all without hesitation. Something gripped my heart, and I was overcome with the feeling that "if he can know our doctrine that well, so can I." After attending several of these debates, I began my quest for doctrinal knowledge and understanding.

By age 14, I had compiled eight typed pages explaining why

we baptize in Jesus' name. Three years later, during the summer between my junior and senior years in high school, I was invited to be the guest on a Christian radio talk show in Dallas, Texas, debating the subject of baptism. Within 10 years of that, God helped me to convert a Trinitarian pastor, baptizing his entire family and a number of his former members! Now, all these years later, the Lord has blessed me to be a part of a revival of Biblical proportions where hundreds upon hundreds are coming to the knowledge of the truth!

I only relate these things for the purpose of showing how Apostolic doctrine has been the focal point of my life and ministry for many years. I am quite certain there are those who will find what I write to be elementary, and I am fine with that. I do not claim to be producing a doctoral thesis filled with profundities twice profounded. I am just a man with a strong passion for the truth who wants to help others comprehend it, receive it, believe it, obey it, and, most of all, love it!

There is a difference between knowledge and understanding. A person can have knowledge of certain facts, but not necessarily understand the meaning of those facts. For example, many people possess the knowledge that $E=mc^2$. Many of those same individuals, however, have no understanding of what those symbols actually mean.

I hope the contents of this book will do more than simply provide you with a knowledge of the subject at hand. I hope it will also give you a very thorough understanding.

It is my sincere prayer that God will use this book for His glory and that many will receive a revelation of truth as a result of having read it. If even one person is convinced, convicted, or converted, it will have been worth my time and effort.

CHAPTER 1
TRUTH VERSUS TRADITION

I am going to do something that I am sure the experts (whomever they might be) would caution me against. I am going to open this first chapter (and, therefore, this book) with a question that might make some people flinch. The question is this: *Do you KNOW you are saved, or do you just THINK you are saved?*

The reason I ask this question is because Jesus said that on Judgment Day, MANY would stand before Him totally deceived about the condition of their souls. They would be SO convinced of their salvation that they would literally argue with God Himself about their spiritual status.

Matthew 7:21-23
Not every one that saith unto me, Lord, Lord, shall enter into the kingdom of heaven; but he that doeth the will of my Father which is in heaven. ²²Many will say to me in that day, Lord, Lord, have we not prophesied in thy name? and in thy name have cast out devils? and in thy name done many wonderful works? ²³And then will I profess unto them, I never knew you: depart from me, ye

that work iniquity.

Please note also that these are NOT people in pagan religions. Rather, these are people who are doing things in Jesus' name!

Thus, it IS possible for a person to believe with all their heart that they are saved and yet find out on Judgment Day that they were not. None of us want to fall into that category – we need to be absolutely certain we are saved!

Perhaps that is one reason Peter instructed us to not take our salvation for granted. Instead, we must "make sure" that we are saved.

2 Peter 1:10
Wherefore the rather, brethren, give diligence
to make your calling and election sure: for if ye
do these things, ye shall never fall:

The question before us, then, is how those of whom Jesus spoke could have been so deceived as to truly believe they were saved when, in fact, they were not? I can only think of one answer – *tradition.* Evidently, they were basing their salvation on things they had been taught and had never searched the Scriptures for themselves!

There are many ways to define the word "tradition." Here are a few: (a) Statements, beliefs, legends, customs, information, etc., which has been handed down from generation to generation, especially by word of mouth or by example; (b) A way of thinking or acting that is based upon long-established or inherited ideas and/or philosophies; (c) A pattern of culture, beliefs, or practices which has become common among a particular group. Tradition can also be defined as some precept or custom not commanded in the written law, but which people themselves feel bound to observe.

For the sake of this book, when dealing with religious traditions, I am talking about teachings that claim to be based on

Scripture but are actually ideas that either have no Biblical base or are directly contrary to what the Bible actually says. With that in mind, let me be clear – not EVERY tradition is wrong.

If that is true, how do we know which traditions to keep and which to avoid? Thankfully, the Apostle Paul answered that question – at least in part.

2 Thessalonians 2:15

Therefore, brethren, stand fast, and hold the traditions which ye have been taught, whether by word, or our epistle.

Thus, we see that IF the tradition is truly based on the Scripture OR comes directly from the Apostles themselves, that tradition is good and should be continued. Therefore, we must recognize that any time one of our traditions is contrary to the Scripture, we are obligated to reject our tradition and embrace the Bible.

Please understand this is true even if the overwhelming majority of people believe some tradition that is contrary to Scripture. Regardless of how many people affirm something that goes against the Bible, the Word of God is ALWAYS right! In fact, even if EVERYONE disagrees with the Bible, it is STILL right!

Romans 3:4

God forbid: yea, let God be true, but every man a liar; as it is written, That thou mightest be justified in thy sayings, and mightest overcome when thou art judged.

This should cause us to recognize that a problem clearly exists when people choose to believe their traditions over the truth of God's Word. Jesus Himself warned against this.

Mark 7:7-8

Howbeit in vain do they worship me, teaching for doctrines the commandments of men. ⁸For laying aside the commandment of God, ye hold the tradition of men, as the washing of pots and cups: and many other such like things ye do.

In my more than 40 years of ministry, I have discovered that most people who call themselves Christians have come to adopt certain teachings as being scriptural, when in fact they are merely traditional. These people have simply never taken the time to search the Scriptures for themselves.

There are a number of "traditions" which have been handed down through the years, and are now being taught as "truth" by the many Christians. This is in spite of the fact that the Bible either does not state it to be true, or clearly shows it is not true. I will not take the time to look at all of them in this chapter, but I will discuss a couple of the most glaring ones.

EXAMPLE #1: How many wise men went to the manger when Jesus was born?

According to tradition, there were three. However, it is important that we find out what the Scriptures say.

Matthew 2:1-2

Now when Jesus was born in Bethlehem of Judaea in the days of Herod the king, behold, there came wise men from the east to Jerusalem, ²Saying, Where is he that is born King of the Jews? for we have seen his star in the east, and are come to worship him.

Interestingly, the Bible does not specify a number – it only says there were "wise *men*" (plural). It could have been any number above one. We do not know. The tradition that teaches there were three is based on the gifts they gave the Christ child.

Matthew 2:11

And when they were come into the house, they saw the young child with Mary his mother, and fell down, and worshipped him: and when they had opened their treasures, they presented unto him gifts; gold, and frankincense, and myrrh.

Notice, however, that although three KINDS of gifts were mentioned, the actual NUMBER of gifts is not identified. There could have been five golden gifts and twelve containers of frankincense and/or myrrh. Tradition, however, has taken the three TYPES of gifts and extrapolated that into three wise men, each giving one gift of the types listed.

It should also be noted that, even if there were just three gifts, that does not mean there had to be three men giving them. Two men – or twenty men – could have given three gifts collectively.

Furthermore, the number of wise men is not the ONLY tradition that has been handed down in this story. Regardless of how many wise men there actually were, the Bible does not indicate that they went to the manger – in fact, it CLEARLY says they went somewhere OTHER than the manger.

Matthew 2:11

And when they were come into the house, they saw the young child with Mary his mother, and fell down, and worshipped him: and when they had opened their treasures, they presented unto him gifts; gold, and frankincense, and myrrh.

Notice that they came into the HOUSE. Luke 2:7 lets us know that Mary and Joseph had found no accommodation in a house, so the Baby had to be born in a stable or stall among the animals.

Notice also that they saw "the young child" (a totally different Greek word than "babe" – which the shepherds were told to find – this word literally means "a toddler"). What the wise men found was NOT a newborn in a manger. They found a toddler in a house!

In fact, it is very probable that Jesus was two years old when the wise men came. Why do I say that? Because of what the Bible says concerning what Herod did.

> ### Matthew 2:16
> *Then Herod, when he saw that he was mocked of the wise men, was exceeding wroth, and sent forth, and slew all the children that were in Bethlehem, and in all the coasts thereof, from two years old and under, according to the time which he had diligently enquired of the wise men.*

Herod chose to kill the babies that were two years old and under BECAUSE that was when the star first appeared to the wise men! If the star appeared when Jesus was born, then He was two by the time the wise men found him.

Thus, our long-held belief that taught us there were three wise men at the stable in Bethlehem is NOT based upon Biblical truth. Rather, it is a tradition many have come to believe as though it were truth.

EXAMPLE #2: How many of each kind of animal did Noah take on the ark?

All of our lives, we have been told that Noah took two of each kind of animal on the ark. We have heard it in Sunday School. We have sung songs about it. We have seen drawings and paintings that depicted it. In every case, there have always been only two. However, is that what the Scripture says?

> ### Genesis 7:1-3
> *And the LORD said unto Noah, Come thou and all thy house into the ark; for thee have I seen righteous before me in this generation. [2]Of every*

clean beast thou shalt take to thee by sevens, the
male and his female: and of beasts that are not
clean by two, the male and his female. ³Of fowls
also of the air by sevens, the male and the female;
to keep seed alive upon the face of all the earth.

While tradition has repeatedly told us there were two of each kind of animal, the Bible tells us that some were taken "by sevens" (some translations say "seven pairs" or fourteen)! Unlike the traditions surrounding the story of the Wise Men (which is based on supposition), this tradition is directly contradictory to the actual Biblical account!

Please consider this: If tradition has led people astray on things this simple – AND so clearly stated in scripture – how much more of their tradition is in error? I submit to you that a LOT of teachings in Christian churches today are nothing more than incorrect traditions being handed down as truth. Furthermore, some VERY important doctrines have been adopted based solely on tradition, and have absolutely no basis in the truth.

Earlier, I pointed out that there will be those who are so convinced they are saved that they will actually argue with the Lord on Judgment Day. I then went on to state that their deception was apparently the result of tradition.

In order to prove what caused these people to be so deceived, let us go back to the passage in question and continue the narrative. By looking at the verses which follow that incident, we get a better understanding of the process that brought about their deception.

Matthew 7:24-27

Therefore whosoever heareth these sayings of
mine, and doeth them, I will liken him unto a wise
man, which built his house upon a rock: ²⁵And the
rain descended, and the floods came, and the
winds blew, and beat upon that house; and it fell

not: for it was founded upon a rock. ^{26}And every one that heareth these sayings of mine, and doeth them not, shall be likened unto a foolish man, which built his house upon the sand: ^{27}And the rain descended, and the floods came, and the winds blew, and beat upon that house; and it fell: and great was the fall of it.

In this parable, Jesus taught that the difference between wisdom and folly – and, by context, salvation and rejection – hinges STRICTLY on OBEDIENCE to God's Word. The foolish man refused to obey the Word, and his house crumbled.

Do you remember what Jesus said to those who believed they were saved but were not? What was the REASON He gave them as to WHY they were lost?

Matthew 7:22-23

Many will say to me in that day, Lord, Lord, have we not prophesied in thy name? and in thy name have cast out devils? and in thy name done many wonderful works? ^{23}And then will I profess unto them, I never knew you: depart from me, ye that work iniquity.

Jesus told them they were guilty of "iniquity." The Greek word used here literally means "without law," or "transgression of the law." The reason these people (who had prophesied, cast out devils, and "done many wonderful works" – all in Jesus' name!) were lost was because they failed to obey the Bible. It is very possible that they simply embraced the traditions they had been handed and never took the time to find out what the Word actually told them to do.

How, then, do we know what is truth and what is tradition? That, my friends, is what we need to find out.

There are some things that MUST be established in

determining what is truth. We do not want to take a chance on simply adhering to a tradition.

During his examination of Christ, Pontius Pilate asked a very important question. As far as I am concerned, it is THE question of the ages!

John 18:38

Pilate saith unto him, What is truth? And when he had said this, he went out again unto the Jews, and saith unto them, I find in him no fault at all.

Personally, I find it somewhat ironic that Pilate would ask that question on this particular day. Only the night before, Jesus had provided the answer during His discourse to His disciples in the Upper Room.

John 17:17

Sanctify them through thy truth: thy word is truth.

Jesus defined for us the ONLY source of absolute truth. It is the Word of God.

If we really want truth, we cannot look to denominational writings, nor to the words of contemporary men. We must look SOLELY to the Word of God!

The reason the Word of God is so essential to us is two-fold. First, Jesus said that we will be judged by the Word of God.

John 12:48

He that rejecteth me, and receiveth not my words, hath one that judgeth him: the word that I have spoken, the same shall judge him in the last day.

I believe we can read of John seeing this happen when he was granted a vision of the Great White Throne Judgment. Notice there was more than the Book of Life that was opened.

Revelation 20:12-15

And I saw the dead, small and great, stand before God; and the books were opened: and another book was opened, which is the book of life: and the dead were judged out of those things which were written in the books, according to their works. [13]And the sea gave up the dead which were in it; and death and hell delivered up the dead which were in them: and they were judged every man according to their works. [14]And death and hell were cast into the lake of fire. This is the second death. [15]And whosoever was not found written in the book of life was cast into the lake of fire.

Not only was the Book of Life opened, but the "books" (plural) were also opened. Furthermore, every man was judged by "those things which were written in the books." Because of Jesus' statement in John 12:48, it is my contention that the "books" out of which we will be judged are the 66 books we call the Bible.

The second reason why the Word of God is so important to us should be obvious. You see, Jesus Christ IS the Word of God.

John 1:1

In the beginning was the Word, and the Word was with God, and the Word was God.

John 1:14

And the Word was made flesh, and dwelt among us, (and we beheld his glory, the glory as of the only begotten of the Father,) full of grace and truth.

If, therefore, we are going to try to discern the difference between truth and error, we must find our answers in the Bible. Furthermore, there is another, more specific key that helps us distinguish between truth and error. It was given to us by the Apostle John.

1 John 4:6

We are of God: he that knoweth God heareth us; he that is not of God heareth not us. Hereby know we the spirit of truth, and the spirit of error.

This Scripture plainly tells us truth and error are determined on the basis of whether or not a doctrine lines up with that which was taught by the Apostles themselves. Whatever we believe concerning any particular Biblical subject, it should never contradict what the Apostles said.

John was not the only one who said this, by the way. Paul confirmed this fact.

Galatians 1:8-9

But though we, or an angel from heaven, preach any other gospel unto you than that which we have preached unto you, let him be accursed. ⁹As we said before, so say I now again, If any man preach any other gospel unto you than that ye have received, let him be accursed.

Thus, regardless of WHO teaches a particular doctrine (or HOW MANY believe it to be true), it is ONLY true if it is in agreement with what the Apostles taught. Any other message is false, and any other messenger is cursed!

In summary, it is eternally important that we reject "traditional teachings" in favor of scriptural truths. The writer of Proverbs warned us about the danger of following a way that only "seems right."

Proverbs 14:12

There is a way which seemeth right unto a man, but the end thereof are the ways of death.

I opened this chapter with a very direct question about whether you know you are saved. With regard to that, let me ask you this: Is the way you are going right, or does it just *seem* right?

It is easy to get trapped in tradition when we do something only because it seems right. We cannot MERELY rely on what seems right, whether it is what we think, believe, or feel, or what we were told by relatives, our Sunday School teacher, our preacher, priest, or rabbi, or what we read in some book. Rather, it is important that we find the answers in the word of God.

John 5:39

Search the scriptures; for in them ye think ye have eternal life: and they are they which testify of me.

CHAPTER 2

THE IMPORTANCE OF THE APOSTLES' DOCTRINE

For many years now, I have been hearing the ecumenical cry of, "Let's forget about doctrine and just love one another." Others have claimed doctrine is simply a way of dividing people who should be united. Evidently, many people believe the term "doctrine" is synonymous for "denominational ideology." Nothing could be further from the truth.

The word "doctrine" is translated from a Greek word which simply means "instruction" or "teaching." However, as it is used in the New Testament, it refers to a specific teaching which God clearly does not want us to abandon. I will endeavor to prove that statement through the use of Scripture.

All four of the Gospel writers made reference to Jesus' doctrine. (See Matthew 7:28, Mark 1:22, Luke 4:32, and John 7:16, *et al*.) Jesus clearly stated in John 7:16 that the doctrine He taught was not something He (as a man) concocted on His own. Rather, it originated with the Father (the Spirit which indwelt Him).

John 7:16
Jesus answered them, and said, My doctrine is not mine, but his that sent me.

Luke tells us that the early church "continued stedfastly in the Apostles' doctrine" (Acts 2:42). The Apostles were accused of having "filled Jerusalem" with their doctrine (Acts 5:28).

Obviously, doctrine was important to Jesus and His disciples. It was also important to the Apostle Paul. Consider just a few of the things he wrote on the subject.

Romans 16:17

Now I beseech you, brethren, mark them which cause divisions and offences contrary to the doctrine which ye have learned; and avoid them.

Ephesians 4:14

That we henceforth be no more children, tossed to and fro, and carried about with every wind of doctrine, by the sleight of men, and cunning craftiness, whereby they lie in wait to deceive;

1 Timothy 1:3

As I besought thee to abide still at Ephesus, when I went into Macedonia, that thou mightest charge some that they teach no other doctrine,

1 Timothy 1:10

For whoremongers, for them that defile themselves with mankind, for menstealers, for liars, for perjured persons, and if there be any other thing that is contrary to sound doctrine;

1 Timothy 4:13

Till I come, give attendance to reading, to exhortation, to doctrine.

1 Timothy 4:16

Take heed unto thyself, and unto the doctrine; continue in them: for in doing this thou shalt both save thyself, and them that hear thee.

2 Timothy 4:2

Preach the word; be instant in season, out of season; reprove, rebuke, exhort with all longsuffering and doctrine.

I could go on listing many more verses in which Paul stressed the importance – yea, the necessity – of doctrine. Again, however, I want to point out that it is not just *any* doctrine. As I pointed out in the first chapter, it must be the doctrine which was taught by the Apostles.

It should be obvious that men can twist the Scriptures and make them mean things they were never intended to mean. That is why Paul instructs us to "rightly divide" the Bible.

2 Timothy 2:15

Study to shew thyself approved unto God, a workman that needeth not to be ashamed, rightly dividing the word of truth.

We will spend more time discussing this verse in the next chapter, but for now, let us consider the proper "divisions" of the Bible. To begin with, we have the Old Testament and the New Testament.

A "testament" is a will or covenant; thus, we have an "old covenant" which was made with the Jewish people, and a "new covenant" which is available to "whosoever will." I do not intend to go into detail about the right way to divide the "old covenant" in this chapter (or even in this book). Instead, I want to focus for a few moments on the four basic divisions of the "new covenant" (i.e., the New Testament).

First, there are the Gospels. These four books basically provide the biography of Jesus Christ. They generally begin somewhere around His birth and end somewhere around His death, burial, and resurrection.

Second, there is the Book of Acts. It is a book of history which provides a detailed account of the actions of the Lord's handpicked successors. In it, we also find the instances where these men preached to the lost. As a result, we can read about individuals being saved and churches being established.

Third, we have the Epistles. These are the books of Romans through Jude. They are letters written for the purpose of strengthening the Churches and/or individuals who were already saved.

The fourth division is the Book of Revelation. This book is generally symbolic (though not entirely). For the most part, it contains prophecies concerning the future and the end of the world. It also gives us glimpses into Heaven and the afterlife.

Recognizing these divisions and their scope is important information which will come in handy as this book unfolds. Before coming back to it, however, I want to ask you to think about something.

Let us consider for a few moments the extreme importance a foundation has to any building. The real strength (and stability) of the structure is wholly dependent upon the quality of the foundation. The fact of the matter is that most problems which are visibly wrong (in a structural sense) are actually due to a problem with the foundation. Obviously, we MUST have a good foundation.

With regards to the Christian church, the Bible itself clearly tells us what our foundation is. We find Jesus referencing it after Simon Peter's great confession of Christ's identity.

Matthew 16:15-19

He saith unto them, But whom say ye that I am?
16 And Simon Peter answered and said, Thou art the Christ, the Son of the living God. 17 And Jesus answered and said unto him, Blessed art thou, Simon Barjona: for flesh and blood hath not revealed it unto thee, but my Father which is in heaven. 18 And I say also unto thee, That thou art Peter, and upon this rock I will build my church; and the gates of hell shall not prevail against it. 19 And I will give unto thee the keys of the kingdom

*of heaven: and whatsoever thou shalt bind on
earth shall be bound in heaven: and whatsoever
thou shalt loose on earth shall be loosed in
heaven.*

When Jesus said, "Upon this rock I will build my church," this was unquestionably a reference to the foundation upon which the church would be built. It should be noted, however, that He was NOT referring to Peter as the foundation.

The name "Peter" comes from the Greek word "petros," but the word used to identify the "rock" upon which the church is built is "petra." "Petros" simply means a rock (or, more accurately, a pebble or small stone), but "petra" refers to a large stone or boulder.

When Jesus spoke of that upon which His church would be built, He was referring to the "rock" of the revelation Peter had been given. Therefore, the first thing we learn about the foundation of the church is that it involves the revelation given to the Apostles. This concept is confirmed in the Book of Ephesians.

Ephesians 2:19-20

*Now therefore ye are no more strangers and
foreigners, but fellowcitizens with the saints, and
of the household of God; [20]And are built upon the
foundation of the Apostles and prophets, Jesus
Christ himself being the chief corner stone;*

Thus, we see that our foundation is "two-fold": first, there were the prophets (in the Old Testament); then came the Apostles (in the New Testament) who built on what the prophets had said. Furthermore, these two sides are held together by the "cornerstone" – Jesus Christ!

Inasmuch as we know the prophets and Apostles make up our foundation, we can safely conclude that WHATEVER the prophets and Apostles said is TRUE! In fact, the Scripture tells us that these men did not even speak from their own opinions, but they were "moved upon" by God's Spirit.

2 Peter 1:20-21

Knowing this first, that no prophecy of the scripture is of any private interpretation. [21]For the prophecy came not in old time by the will of man: but holy men of God spake as they were moved by the Holy Ghost.

We also understand that ALL Scripture was inspired by God Himself. Paul said as much to Timothy.

2 Timothy 3:16

All scripture is given by inspiration of God, and is profitable for doctrine, for reproof, for correction, for instruction in righteousness:

Since our foundation is built on what the Apostles said, we should strive to pay special attention to their words. This is especially true when they are speaking to those who are lost.

Let's face it. There are many men today who CLAIM to have been "sent by God." Sometimes it is hard to know whether they were or were not. However, we know without a doubt that the Apostles WERE sent by God because the Bible says they were!

John 17:17-20

Sanctify them through thy truth: thy word is truth. [18]As thou hast sent me into the world, even so have I also sent them into the world. [19]And for their sakes I sanctify myself, that they also might be sanctified through the truth. [20]Neither pray I for these alone, but for them also which shall believe on me through their word;

In this passage, Jesus specifically said He had sent them. Furthermore, Jesus ALSO said *we* would believe on Him "through

THEIR [the Apostles'] word." Since the man Christ Jesus never left a written word behind, we are completely dependent upon the writings of His followers to know what He said and did.

It does not matter how popular a man is or even how large his congregation and/or following may be. Paul made it very clear that ANY doctrine other than what he and the other Apostles preached would be cursed by God.

> ### Galatians 1:6-12
>
> *I marvel that ye are so soon removed from him that called you into the grace of Christ unto another gospel: ⁷Which is not another; but there be some that trouble you, and would pervert the gospel of Christ. ⁸But though we, or an angel from heaven, preach any other gospel unto you than that which we have preached unto you, let him be accursed. ⁹As we said before, so say I now again, If any man preach any other gospel unto you than that ye have received, let him be accursed. ¹⁰For do I now persuade men, or God? or do I seek to please men? for if I yet pleased men, I should not be the servant of Christ. ¹¹But I certify you, brethren, that the gospel which was preached of me is not after man. ¹²For I neither received it of man, neither was I taught it, but by the revelation of Jesus Christ.*

Paul had the assurance the doctrine he taught was correct because he received it by direct revelation from God. Because of this fact, he warned us to "mark" anyone who preached something different than what he and the other Apostles preached.

> ### Romans 16:17-18
>
> *Now I beseech you, brethren, mark them which cause divisions and offences contrary to the doctrine which ye have learned; and avoid them.*

> *[18]For they that are such serve not our Lord Jesus Christ, but their own belly; and by good words and fair speeches deceive the hearts of the simple.*

Paul even instructed the church at Rome (and, by extension, EVERY church) to "avoid" anyone who is teaching anything different than what the church had already learned. In order to see what they had "learned," you must keep reading down through verse 25.

Romans 16:25

> *Now to him that is of power to stablish you according to my gospel, and the preaching of Jesus Christ, according to the revelation of the mystery, which was kept secret since the world began,*

Notice that Paul spoke of "my gospel" (the message which he and the other Apostles preached). It is only the gospel preached by the Apostles that has power and authority.

As we pointed out in the previous chapter, John the Beloved said that the message of the Apostles is the benchmark by which all doctrines should be measured. Any other message is in "error."

1 John 4:6

> *We are of God: he that knoweth God heareth us; he that is not of God heareth not us. Hereby know we the spirit of truth, and the spirit of error.*

He also told us that ANYONE who preaches ANYTHING other than what the Apostles preached should not be welcomed into our homes. Nor should we "bid them godspeed" (which means to wish them well, or greet them with joy).

2 John 1:9-11

> *Whosoever transgresseth, and abideth not in the doctrine of Christ, hath not God. He that*

abideth in the doctrine of Christ, he hath both the Father and the Son. [10]If there come any unto you, and bring not this doctrine, receive him not into your house, neither bid him God speed: [11]For he that biddeth him God speed is partaker of his evil deeds.

There are many doctrines in the world today. Trying to decipher who is right and who is wrong may seem like a daunting task. However, it is really not difficult at all. All we have to do is compare a doctrine to what the Apostles taught, and we will know immediately if it is truth or error.

One reason we can be certain that the message of the Apostles is accurate is because Jesus Himself told them what to preach. Furthermore, the Bible says He made sure they understood it!

Luke 24:44-45

And he said unto them, These are the words which I spake unto you, while I was yet with you, that all things must be fulfilled, which were written in the law of Moses, and in the prophets, and in the psalms, concerning me. [45]Then opened he their understanding, that they might understand the scriptures,

First, notice in verse 45, the Bible says He "opened their understanding." There is no way anyone with an honest heart can say these men were confused about what Jesus wanted them to teach or preach. To do so is to reject the plain statement found in the Scripture.

Second, it is important that we pay attention to exactly what He told them to preach. This list of important parts to the message Jesus gave them is found in verses 46-49.

Luke 24:46-49

And said unto them, Thus it is written, and thus it behoved Christ to suffer, and to rise from the dead the third day: ⁴⁷And that repentance and remission of sins should be preached in his name among all nations, beginning at Jerusalem. ⁴⁸And ye are witnesses of these things. ⁴⁹And, behold, I send the promise of my Father upon you: but tarry ye in the city of Jerusalem, until ye be endued with power from on high.

Here we find three things the Apostles were told to preach. Jesus said they should preach: (1) repentance; (2) remission of sins in Jesus' name; and (3) the promise of the Father. We also find that they were to start in Jerusalem.

Rest assured these men did EXACTLY what they were told to do. Pay close attention to the following Scriptures.

First, we know they went to Jerusalem. The Bible is clear about this.

Acts 1:12-13

Then returned they unto Jerusalem from the mount called Olivet, which is from Jerusalem a sabbath day's journey. ¹³And when they were come in, they went up into an upper room, where abode both Peter, and James, and John, and Andrew, Philip, and Thomas, Bartholomew, and Matthew, James the son of Alphaeus, and Simon Zelotes, and Judas the brother of James.

While in Jerusalem, they preached the first message to a lost crowd after the birth of the church. That message included the three things Jesus had commanded them to preach.

Acts 2:36-39

Therefore let all the house of Israel know

assuredly, that God hath made that same Jesus, whom ye have crucified, both Lord and Christ. ³⁷Now when they heard this, they were pricked in their heart, and said unto Peter and to the rest of the Apostles, Men and brethren, what shall we do? ³⁸Then Peter said unto them, Repent, and be baptized every one of you in the name of Jesus Christ for the remission of sins, and ye shall receive the gift of the Holy Ghost. ³⁹For the promise is unto you, and to your children, and to all that are afar off, even as many as the Lord our God shall call.

(1) Jesus commanded them to preach repentance, and Peter said, "Repent!"

(2) Jesus commanded them to preach remission of sins in His name, and Peter preached, "Be baptized every one of you in the name of Jesus Christ for the remission of sins."

(3) Jesus commanded them to preach the promise of the Father, and Peter preached, "Ye shall receive the gift of the Holy Ghost, for the promise is unto you!"

Before closing this chapter, I think it is important that I point out once again that Jesus insisted this would begin in Jerusalem. The significance of this is found in something Paul said when writing to the church at Galatia.

Galatians 4:26
But Jerusalem which is above is free, which is the mother of us all.

The foundation of the church – the basis for true doctrine – has to come from Jerusalem. That is our "mother." Too many people base their doctrine on ideas that came from Rome. We should not err in doing this. Let us rather trace our teachings to the original church and those who labored to establish it.

I will go into much more detail in explaining the three parts of the message of the Apostles in the chapters that follow. In fact, I will devote an entire chapter to each of these three points.

Before we can understand any of that, however, we must first acknowledge the fact that the message of the Apostles is the foundation upon which the true church is built! No other doctrine can save. No other doctrine is acceptable. We MUST have an Apostolic foundation if we are going to pursue the truth.

CHAPTER 3
RIGHTLY DIVIDING THE WORD

In his First Epistle to Timothy, the Apostle Paul gave explicit instructions to his "son in the Gospel" concerning his handling of the Scriptures. He told him what to do, how to do it, and the reason it mattered.

> **2 Timothy 2:15**
> *Study to shew thyself approved unto God, a workman that needeth not to be ashamed, rightly dividing the word of truth.*

The International Standard Version says, "Do your best to present yourself to God as an approved worker who has nothing to be ashamed of."[1] The same translation says this is accomplished by "handling the word of truth with precision."[1]

In order to handle the Word with precision, there are two things that must be accomplished. First, one must study. Jesus said as much when He commanded His hearers to "search the Scriptures."

---

[1] DAVIDSON PRESS. (2003). *The Holy Bible: International Standard Version : New Testament.* Yorba Linda, CA, Davidson Press.

John 5:39

Search the scriptures; for in them ye think ye have eternal life: and they are they which testify of me.

The Greek word translated "search" literally means to "inquire" or "investigate." The International Standard Version translates it as "examine carefully."[12]

Paul said "the servant of the Lord" must be "apt to teach."

2 Timothy 2:24

And the servant of the Lord must not strive; but be gentle unto all men, apt to teach, patient,

The Amplified Bible translates this phrase as being "a skilled and suitable teacher."[3] This can ONLY be accomplished through STUDY. Simply studying, however, is NOT enough – we must be sure we study PROPERLY.

2 Timothy 2:14-15

Of these things put them in remembrance, charging them before the Lord that they strive not about words to no profit, but to the subverting of the hearers. [15]Study to shew thyself approved unto God, a workman that needeth not to be ashamed, rightly dividing the word of truth.

Dr. Albert Barnes offered an interesting insight into to the phrase, "strive not about words to no profit." He said it was dealing with the "kind of discourse which is not founded in good

---

[2] DAVIDSON PRESS. (2003). *The Holy Bible: International Standard Version : New Testament.* Yorba Linda, CA, Davidson Press.
[3]SIEWERT, F. E. (1958). *The Amplified Bible.* Grand Rapids, MI, Zondervan.

sense."[4]

This brings us to the second essential ingredient for being able to handle the Bible "with precision" – RIGHTLY dividing the Word of Truth. Please understand that the addition of the adverb "rightly" would only have been necessary if it is possible that someone could "wrongly" divide it. Therefore, Paul wanted to be sure that a person avoid "wrongly dividing" the Scriptures, being diligent about "rightly dividing" it instead.

The Bible can be twisted to mean just about anything. In fact, not only CAN it be done, it has been happening for thousands of years! The fact that the Apostle Peter warned about this shows it was happening even in his day.

2 Peter 3:16

> *As also in all his epistles, speaking in them of these things; in which are some things hard to be understood, which they that are unlearned and unstable wrest, as they do also the other scriptures, unto their own destruction.*

The word "wrest" literally means "to torture," or, by extension, "to pervert." Thus, it is possible to take some verse (or partial verse) and "pervert" or twist it so as to make it appear to say something it is not.

Let me give you an example: Suppose you take the phrase written about Judas in Matthew 27:5 that he "went out and hanged himself," and combine it with Jesus' command in Luke 10:37 to "go thou and do likewise." Then, add to that His instruction in John 13:27 which says, "That thou doest, do quickly." By doing this you can establish a doctrine that everyone ought to hurry out

---

[4]BARNES, A., MURPHY, J. G., COOK, F. C., PUSEY, E. B., LEUPOLD, H. C., & FREW, R. (1996). *Barnes' Notes*. Grand Rapids, Michigan: Baker.

and commit suicide!

The problem is, of course, that those verses were never meant to be taken together. Each of them occurs at different times and has a very different application. This is why we must learn to "rightly divide the Word."

In the last chapter, we discussed the basic "divisions" in Biblical study. Within the New Testament, we showed that there are four divisions which should be recognized: (1) the gospels (Matthew, Mark, Luke, and John), which provide the "biography" of Jesus Christ generally beginning somewhere around His birth, and ending somewhere around His death, burial, and resurrection; (2) the Book of Acts, which tells of the actions of the Apostles, providing a thorough examination of their works and words (especially the message they preached to the lost); (3) the Epistles (Romans through Jude), which are letters written to churches and/or individuals who are already saved, providing them with instruction as to how they should live a sanctified life; and (4) The Book of Revelation, which is a book of prophecy foretelling events that are yet to come.

These are simply the basic divisions, however. In order to "rightly divide" the Word, you will need certain "tools" which will allow you to "skillfully handle" the Scriptures. In this chapter, I want to provide you with the necessary tools which will enable you to discover the proper interpretation of a Biblical passage.

These tools will be used throughout the remainder of this book. By recognizing and employing them in your own study, you will readily recognize the truths I will present in chapters 4 through 6.

There are many necessary tools that help in proper Biblical interpretation, and I want to share with you what I consider to be eight of the most important ones. The easy way to remember these eight is to form an acronym: DUCH L PUI.

* Definition – finding the meaning of the words

* Usage – how a particular word is used in the passage in question

* Context – the setting of the Scripture itself (the verses before and after)

* Historical Background – understanding the history of the people, the setting, and the intended audience

* Logic – making sense of the verse

* Precedence – whether this is the first mention of this subject

* Unity – how it fits into the overall picture of the Bible

* Inference – understanding what is implied by the verse

For any tool to function properly, however, one must learn to use it skillfully. What I really want to focus on in this chapter, therefore, is not so much the tools that are needed as the principles which govern the use of those tools.

There are four principles in particular which I present for your consideration. As I have already stated, these are the principles which will be used repeatedly throughout this book. They are:

* The Scripture is of No Private Interpretation

* Always Let Scripture Interpret Scripture

* Consider the Law of First Mention

* Always Require More than One Witness

Principle #1: The Scripture is of No Private Interpretation

In my opinion, the principle I am about to introduce may well be the most important. That is, of course, the reason I am listing it first. It is based on a statement Peter made.

> ### *2 Peter 1:19-21*
> *We have also a more sure word of prophecy; whereunto ye do well that ye take heed, as unto a light that shineth in a dark place, until the day*

> *dawn, and the day star arise in your hearts:*
> *[20]Knowing this first, that no prophecy of the*
> *scripture is of any private interpretation. [21]For*
> *the prophecy came not in old time by the will of*
> *man: but holy men of God spake as they were*
> *moved by the Holy Ghost.*

During the dark ages, the religious leaders used this verse to convince people that they could not personally understand the Scriptures. Their explanation was that, inasmuch as the common man was not trained in the original languages or manners and customs of ancient times, they did not have the knowledge or wisdom to try to understand (let alone explain) what any passage of Scripture meant.

Of course, this is NOT what Peter meant when he said that no "scripture is of any private interpretation." In order to understand this verse and its true meaning, let us consider the way this verse is translated in other versions.

> **The Amplified Bible:** *"Yet first you must*
> *understand this, that no prophecy of Scripture is*
> *a matter of any personal or private or special*
> *interpretation (loosening, solving). [21]For no*
> *prophecy ever originated because some man*
> *willed it to do so—it never came by human*
> *impulse, but men spoke from God who were*
> *borne along (moved and impelled) by the Holy*
> *Spirit."[5]*

> **The New American Standard Bible:** *"But*
> *know this first of all, that no prophecy of*
> *Scripture is a matter of one's own interpretation,*
> *for no prophecy was ever made an act of human*

---

[5] SIEWERT, F. E. (1958). *The Amplified Bible*. Grand Rapids, Mich, Zondervan.

will, but men moved by the Holy Spirit spoke from God. "[6]

Thus, it should be clear that Peter's intent was not to discourage us from trying to understand the Bible. Rather, he wanted to show us that we cannot simply devise an interpretation that we like (or that fits our views). Instead, we must find the interpretation which God intended.

We need to understand that even though there may be many applications which can be made from a passage of Scripture, there is only one interpretation. We must concede the fact that GOD'S is the only true interpretation!

Unfortunately, too many people use the Bible like a drunkard uses a lamp post – it is more for support than for illumination! Rather than trying to make the Bible say something that supports our predetermined ideas, we must let the Scripture illuminate our minds – even if this means our ideas are proven wrong in the process!

Furthermore, just because a majority of people embrace a particular interpretation, that does not make it the correct one. We must adopt the attitude Paul had with regard to whether the majority is always right.

Romans 3:4

God forbid: yea, let God be true, but every man a liar; as it is written, That thou mightest be justified in thy sayings, and mightest overcome when thou art judged.

The Bible expresses God's thoughts, will, and words – and not man's. Therefore, we must respect it enough to study it until we are able to fully grasp exactly what He intended to tell us!

---

[6] (1972). *New American Standard Bible: New Testament.* Longview, Tex, Word for the World.

God's Word will never change. Therefore, the MEANING will never change!

Psalms 119:89

For ever, O LORD, thy word is settled in heaven.

The reason I said earlier that I believe this is the most important principle of interpretation is because it establishes the fact that there is only one PROPER interpretation. If there are many interpretations, then it matters little how we arrive at the meaning. If, on the other hand, there is only ONE interpretation, we must practice due diligence in finding that one meaning.

Principle #2: Let Scripture Interpret Scripture

For centuries, many denominations have held to a belief that is identified as "Sola Scriptura," which means "only scripture."

Ligonier Ministries offers the following information on this:

> *Sola Scriptura simply means that all truth necessary for our salvation and spiritual life is taught ... in Scripture. ... Scripture is therefore the perfect and only standard of spiritual truth, revealing infallibly all that we must believe in order to be saved and all that we must do in order to glorify God. ... "The whole counsel of God, concerning all things necessary for his own glory, man's salvation, faith, and life, is either expressly set down in scripture, or by good and necessary consequence may be deduced from scripture: unto which nothing at any time is to be added, whether by new revelations of the Spirit, or traditions of men."*[7]

---

[7] https://www.ligonier.org/blog/what-does-sola-scriptura-mean/

The Psalmist declared God's Word has ALWAYS been true. He also asserted that it will ALWAYS continue to be so!

Psalms 119:160

Thy word is true from the beginning: and every one of thy righteous judgments endureth for ever.

Furthermore, Jesus Himself testified as to the veracity of Scripture. According to the Lord Himself, the Bible does not just contain truth – it IS truth!

John 17:17

Sanctify them through thy truth: thy word is truth.

Paul declared that we can trust the Bible in its entirety. He emphatically stated that ALL Scripture was given by God.

2 Timothy 3:16

All scripture is given by inspiration of God, and is profitable for doctrine, for reproof, for correction, for instruction in righteousness:

The phrase "inspiration of God" literally means "God-breathed." This, of course, directly concurs with Peter's statement that men spoke as they were moved by God's Spirit to do so.

With this in mind, we must recognize the Bible is not only the best source of information; it is also the best source of interpretation! Therefore, any time we encounter a verse we do not understand, we should seek FIRST to find another scripture which will help us find its meaning.

During the temptation of Christ, the devil tried to twist the Scriptures. In order to counter his wrong interpretation, Jesus used more Scripture!

Matthew 4:6

And saith unto him, If thou be the Son of God, cast thyself down: for it is written, He shall give

*his angels charge concerning thee: and in their
hands they shall bear thee up, lest at any time
thou dash thy foot against a stone.*

The devil was quoting from Psalm 91. When you read the passage to which he referred, you see that the problem was not in the way he quoted it.

Psalms 91:11-12

*For he shall give his angels charge over thee,
to keep thee in all thy ways. ^{12}They shall bear thee
up in their hands, lest thou dash thy foot against
a stone.*

The problem was in the way he applied it. Notice, however, Jesus' response.

Matthew 4:7

*Jesus said unto him, It is written again, Thou
shalt not tempt the Lord thy God.*

By using another Scripture, Jesus showed that the enemy had taken the verses from Psalms out of context and had given them a wrong interpretation. Inasmuch as one verse cannot contradict another, it is clear that the devil's application was not proper.

This is not the only time Jesus used Scripture to explain other Scriptures. He did the same thing when confronted by the Pharisees with a probing question.

Matthew 19:3-6

*The Pharisees also came unto him, tempting
him, and saying unto him, Is it lawful for a man
to put away his wife for every cause? ^{4}And he
answered and said unto them, Have ye not read,
that he which made them at the beginning made
them male and female, ^{5}And said, For this cause
shall a man leave father and mother, and shall*

cleave to his wife: and they twain shall be one flesh? ⁶Wherefore they are no more twain, but one flesh. What therefore God hath joined together, let not man put asunder.

Here, Jesus went back to Genesis 2 to explain the subject of divorce. He was then asked about a related scripture.

Matthew 19:7

They say unto him, Why did Moses then command to give a writing of divorcement, and to put her away?

This is a clear reference to the Book of Deuteronomy. It was there that Moses outlined the rules concerning divorce.

Deuteronomy 24:1

When a man hath taken a wife, and married her, and it come to pass that she find no favour in his eyes, because he hath found some uncleanness in her: then let him write her a bill of divorcement, and give it in her hand, and send her out of his house.

Follow with me: first, Jesus was asked a question. Second, He replied with a Scripture. Third, His inquisitors responded with a Scripture of their own. Finally, in order to explain that verse, Jesus reminded them of the verses He had already addressed.

Matthew 19:8

He saith unto them, Moses because of the hardness of your hearts suffered you to put away your wives: but from the beginning it was not so.

In other words, even though Moses allowed it, divorce was not God's intention from the beginning. Thus, the ultimate interpretation was based on the consistent application of Bible verses.

I will not take the time to show the many examples of the Apostles using this same method throughout the epistles. Nevertheless, suffice it to say they understood and practiced the principle of using the scriptures to interpret the scriptures!

Principle #3: Consider the Law of First Mention

Most Bible scholars agree that the very first time any doctrine or topic is mentioned in the Scripture, that subject is generally addressed in such a way as to provide the foundational approach for our understanding. To accomplish this, for instance, the "first mention" might give the subject its most complete and accurate description. This means the idea behind a particular verse may actually have already been provided in a previous passage.

One example of how this works is found in the Book of Genesis. It involves the creation of the world.

In Genesis 1 (the first time creation is mentioned), we learn that God separated light from darkness on the first day; He divided the waters above and below the firmament on the second day; He separated the land from the sea on the third day; He created the stars, sun, and moon on the fourth day; He created sea life and birds on the fifth day; He created land animals and man on the sixth day; and He rested on the seventh day. Obviously, the first mention of creation gives a LOT of details.

There are many other passages throughout both the Old and New Testaments which mention creation, some even stating that it was done in seven days. However, there are NO other scriptures which provide the details of what He created on which day such as is given in the first mention.

For example, consider the reference to creation which is found in Exodus.

Exodus 20:11

For in six days the LORD made heaven and earth, the sea, and all that in them is, and rested

the seventh day: wherefore the LORD blessed the
sabbath day, and hallowed it.

In other passages, we are not even told how many days were involved. Such is the case in a well-known verse in Hebrews.

Hebrews 11:3

Through faith we understand that the worlds
were framed by the word of God, so that things
which are seen were not made of things which do
appear.

The lack of details in later passages does not negate what the first mention says. Rather, it is simply expected that you will base your understanding of these later verses on the details given in the first mention.

This principle not only serves as a "key" to understanding the topic's Biblical concept, but also provides a foundation for its more complete development in later parts of the Bible. Remember how Jesus addressed the subject of divorce? In order to establish His case, Jesus went back to how it was "in the beginning" – in other words, He based His interpretation on the first mention.

Any time we are trying to understand the meaning of a verse, we should always find the first time that subject is mentioned in the Bible. In doing so, we will have a greater understanding of what is happening. At times we will find much more detail in that first mention. We will usually be given important facts. Knowledge of those facts could possibly show us that the way we have been interpreting a verse may not have been accurate.

Principle #4: Always Require More than One Witness

Throughout the Bible, God had one rule regarding how to best determine the validity of an accusation. He made it clear that simply having one person claim to be a witness of some action done by another was not sufficient.

Numbers 35:30

Whoso killeth any person, the murderer shall be put to death by the mouth of witnesses: but one witness shall not testify against any person to cause him to die.

The reason behind this requirement should be obvious – no one wants to be condemned based on the word of just one individual. Doing so would allow anyone with a personal vendetta to bring unfair punishment upon his enemy. Therefore, God required more than one person to be able to testify that they witnessed the alleged offense.

It is interesting to note that this principle is established by the principle itself. It appears to me that God Himself wanted to reiterate how important this principle was.

Deuteronomy 17:6

At the mouth of two witnesses, or three witnesses, shall he that is worthy of death be put to death; but at the mouth of one witness he shall not be put to death.

Deuteronomy 19:15

One witness shall not rise up against a man for any iniquity, or for any sin, in any sin that he sinneth: at the mouth of two witnesses, or at the mouth of three witnesses, shall the matter be established.

Matthew 18:16

But if he will not hear thee, then take with thee one or two more, that in the mouth of two or three witnesses every word may be established.

John 8:17

It is also written in your law, that the testimony of two men is true.

2 Corinthians 13:1

This is the third time I am coming to you. In the mouth of two or three witnesses shall every word be established.

As you can see, there are six separate scriptures which state (or at least allude to) this principle. Thus, the fact that at least "two or three witnesses" are required to establish any truth is itself established by more than one witness!

In establishing any important scriptural truth and/or doctrine, it is important to adopt the practice of requiring at least two scriptures. Otherwise, we cannot be certain our teaching is valid.

Having said this, however, I am NOT implying the scripture is wrong. I am only saying that our interpretation may be wrong!

If you follow this principle, you will recognize that you cannot take a single verse or a part of the verse and use it to ascertain exactly what the Bible says on a given subject. You are required to provide the collaborating, cooperating, and corresponding testimony of at least a second witness.

There is another reason why this principle is so important. The Bible is written in such a way that part of any truth may be in one place, and another part in another place.

Isaiah 28:10

For precept must be upon precept, precept upon precept; line upon line, line upon line; here a little, and there a little:

Therefore, to get the whole truth, these parts have to be put together. "Partial truth" is still error!

Just as a few pieces of a puzzle will not show the whole picture, so using one verse of Scripture taken out of context will not provide enough clarity to determine the full truth. This may be best illustrated in the story of the blind men and the elephant.

It was six men of Indostan, to learning much inclined, who went to see the Elephant (though all of them were blind), that each by observation might satisfy his mind.

The First approach'd the Elephant, and happening to fall against his broad and sturdy side, at once began to bawl: "God bless me! but the Elephant is very like a wall!"

The Second, feeling of the tusk, cried, - "Ho! what have we here, so very round and smooth and sharp? To me 'tis mighty clear, this wonder of an Elephant is very like a spear!"

The Third approach'd the animal, And happening to take the squirming trunk within his hands, thus boldly up and spake: "I see," - quoth he – "the Elephant is very like a snake!"

The Fourth reached out an eager hand, and felt about the knee: "What most this wondrous beast is like is mighty plain," - quoth he, - "'Tis clear enough the Elephant is very like a tree!"

The Fifth, who chanced to touch the ear, said – "E'en the blindest man can tell what this resembles most; deny the fact who can? This marvel of an Elephant is very like a fan!"

The Sixth no sooner had begun about the beast to grope, then, seizing on the swinging tail that fell within his scope, "I see," - quoth he, - "the Elephant is very like a rope!"

And so these men of Indostan disputed loud and long, each in his own opinion exceeding stiff and strong, though each was partly in the right, and all were in the wrong!

MORAL, so, oft in theologic wars the disputants, I ween, rail on in utter ignorance of what each other mean; and prate about an Elephant not one of them has seen![8]

---

[8] SAXE, J. G., DARGIN, P., RYAN, D., & GARLAND, M. (1982). *Six blind men and the elephant.* Dubbo [N.S.W.], Western Region Country Area Program, Western Readers.

So it is with the Word of God. If you take only one verse, you may arrive at a conclusion which is very different from the whole picture. Therefore, ALWAYS look for AT LEAST a second witness to back up your perception of what a verse is supposed to mean. If you cannot find at least one other scripture to support your interpretation, then you need to find a different interpretation because yours is wrong!

As I close this chapter, I want to remind you that I will be employing these principles to uncover truths which to some have long been buried beneath the shroud of tradition. Since "The Scripture is of No Private Interpretation," we will seek to find out exactly what God intends for us to see. We will consistently "Let Scripture Interpret Scripture." When examining a passage, we will "Consider the Law of First Mention" and how it might apply to the topic at hand. Plus, we will "Always Require More than One Witness" to establish any doctrine. By using these four principles on a consistent basis, we are striving to become a "workman that needeth not to be ashamed, rightly dividing the word of truth!" (See 2 Timothy 2:15.)

CHAPTER 4
REPENTANCE

In Chapter 2, we showed you that Jesus gave specific instructions as to the message He expected His disciples to preach. The first thing He mentioned was repentance. Therefore, it is the first step we must take in order to be saved.

Luke 24:46-49

And said unto them, Thus it is written, and thus it behoved Christ to suffer, and to rise from the dead the third day: ⁴⁷And that repentance and remission of sins should be preached in his name among all nations, beginning at Jerusalem. ⁴⁸And ye are witnesses of these things. ⁴⁹And, behold, I send the promise of my Father upon you: but tarry ye in the city of Jerusalem, until ye be endued with power from on high.

There can be no question that Jesus not only *preached about* repentance, He commanded it! He was very clear when He addressed the subject.

Luke 13:2-5

And Jesus answering said unto them, Suppose ye that these Galilaeans were sinners above all the Galilaeans, because they suffered such

things? ³I tell you, Nay: but, except ye repent, ye
shall all likewise perish. ⁴Or those eighteen, upon
whom the tower in Siloam fell, and slew them,
think ye that they were sinners above all men that
dwelt in Jerusalem? ⁵I tell you, Nay: but, except
ye repent, ye shall all likewise perish.

The reason for this is simple. Everyone NEEDS to repent because EVERYONE has sinned!

Romans 3:23

For all have sinned, and come short of the
glory of God;

It is easy for us to try to excuse ourselves because we are "not as bad" as someone else. Some people say, "I have never killed anyone," or "I do not do drugs" in order to justify their "lesser degree" of sinfulness. Nevertheless, ALL have sinned!

Consider this simple illustration: More than 5 million people live in the state of Colorado. Within that state, there are mountains as well as gorges. One person can be in Colorado and be at an elevation of more than 14,000 feet above sea level. However, another person can be in the same state (perhaps at the bottom of the Royal Gorge), and be at a much different elevation. Just because someone is not as "low" or "high" as someone else does not mean they are not in the same state.

In the same way, our "depth" of sin (or lack thereof) makes no different as to our "state." We are all born into one "state:" the "state" of sin.

Psalm 51:5

Behold, I was shapen in iniquity; and in sin did
my mother conceive me.

Compounding the problem of man's sinfulness is the fact of God's holiness. The Bible is replete with verses which state unequivocally that God is holy. Neither time nor space would allow me to list all of them here, but I will give you a few to suffice.

Leviticus 20:7

Sanctify yourselves therefore, and be ye holy: for I am the LORD your God.

Psalm 99:9

Exalt the LORD our God, and worship at his holy hill; for the LORD our God is holy.

1 Peter 1:15-16

But as he which hath called you is holy, so be ye holy in all manner of conversation; [16]Because it is written, Be ye holy; for I am holy.

Holiness is evidently God's PRIMARY attribute. I say this because it seems to be the ONLY attribute the angels around the throne proclaim.

Isaiah 6:3

And one cried unto another, and said, Holy, holy, holy, is the LORD of hosts: the whole earth is full of his glory.

Revelation 4:8

And the four beasts had each of them six wings about him; and they were full of eyes within: and they rest not day and night, saying, Holy, holy, holy, Lord God Almighty, which was, and is, and is to come.

Because we are sinners and God is holy, we must be cleansed before we can make a proper approach unto God. That cleansing process begins with repentance. This is undoubtedly why the scriptures so clearly command it.

Luke 13:2-5

*And Jesus answering said unto them, Suppose
ye that these Galilaeans were sinners above all
the Galilaeans, because they suffered such
things? ³I tell you, Nay: but, except ye repent, ye
shall all likewise perish. ⁴Or those eighteen, upon
whom the tower in Siloam fell, and slew them,
think ye that they were sinners above all men that
dwelt in Jerusalem? ⁵I tell you, Nay: but, except
ye repent, ye shall all likewise perish.*

2 Peter 3:9

*The Lord is not slack concerning his promise,
as some men count slackness; but is longsuffering
to us-ward, not willing that any should perish, but
that all should come to repentance.*

Acts 17:30

*And the times of this ignorance God winked at;
but now commandeth all men every where to
repent:*

The last Scripture I listed is interesting. Pay close attention to
the tense: God winked (past tense), but NOW (present tense)
commands! Also, pay close attention to the mandate: commandeth
– ALL men – EVERY WHERE! There are no exceptions.
Everyone MUST repent!

The second chapter of the Book of Acts provides us with the
events surrounding the birth of the church on the Day of Pentecost.
On the first day of the church's existence, the crowd felt convicted
of their sin and cried out to the Apostles, "What shall we do [to be
saved]?" In response, Peter's FIRST command was "REPENT!"

Acts 2:37-39

*Now when they heard this, they were pricked in
their heart, and said unto Peter and to the rest of*

the Apostles, Men and brethren, what shall we do? ³⁸Then Peter said unto them, Repent, and be baptized every one of you in the name of Jesus Christ for the remission of sins, and ye shall receive the gift of the Holy Ghost. ³⁹For the promise is unto you, and to your children, and to all that are afar off, even as many as the Lord our God shall call.

In the very next chapter, we again find Peter preaching. In this instance, the apostle not only commands repentance, but he makes it clear that the only way to have our sins "blotted out" is to REPENT.

Acts 3:19

Repent ye therefore, and be converted, that your sins may be blotted out, when the times of refreshing shall come from the presence of the Lord;

It should be obvious that repentance is NOT optional. Because of that, it is imperative that we understand what repentance is.

Before explaining what it IS, I want to first explain what it NOT. It should be evident that it is NOT "believing on the Lord" or "accepting the Lord."

Furthermore, it is NOT just saying, "I am sorry for my sins" (although that should be a part of it). In order to prove this, I ask you to consider the following scripture.

Hebrews 12:16-17

Lest there be any fornicator, or profane person, as Esau, who for one morsel of meat sold his birthright. ¹⁷For ye know how that afterward, when he would have inherited the blessing, he was rejected: for he found no place of repentance, though he sought it carefully with tears.

The Bible says that Esau "found no place of repentance." Repentance must be more than simply saying, "I am sorry." Otherwise, please explain why, although he was seeking carefully with tears, he could find no place to speak those words. Obviously, there is more to repentance than a simple apology.

Having addressed what repentance is NOT, let us now turn our attention to discovering – from the Scripture – what it IS. As we do so, we will discover that repentance is a process, with each step predicated on the one before.

We will examine this process (with its succeeding steps) through the remainder of this chapter. Please keep in mind that everything I am telling you comes directly from the Word of God.

In order to truly repent, the first thing we must do is to **see sin from God's perspective.** God sees sin as a cause for death.

Ezekiel 18:20

The soul that sinneth, it shall die. The son shall not bear the iniquity of the father, neither shall the father bear the iniquity of the son: the righteousness of the righteous shall be upon him, and the wickedness of the wicked shall be upon him.

I realize that using this verse will cause some to claim that it is not relevant to those of us who are no longer living under the law. However, I submit to you that this is NOT just an "Old Testament Principle." The Apostle Paul taught the same thing in the New Testament.

Romans 6:23

For the wages of sin is death; but the gift of God is eternal life through Jesus Christ our Lord.

Since God sees sin as carrying the death penalty, He therefore hates it just as any parent hates a disease which threatens the life of their children.

If we see sin from God's perspective, we will realize that, although it IS a product of human nature, we cannot simply dismiss it and overlook it. Sin is not just a "harmless mistake." Rather, it must be dealt with like any fatal disease, for that is EXACTLY what it is (in the spiritual sense).

Seeing sin as the source of spiritual death should bring about the next step in the process of repentance. Knowing how wrong we have been, we should begin to **feel conviction.**

Let us look again at the result of what Peter preached to the crowd at Pentecost. When they realized their sin, they felt conviction.

> ### Acts 2:37
> *Now when they heard this, they were pricked in their heart, and said unto Peter and to the rest of the Apostles, Men and brethren, what shall we do?*

I think it is safe to say that this is what Paul (then called "Saul of Tarsus") had been feeling, and even tried to fight against it. Jesus addressed Paul's conviction when he struck him down on the road to Damascus.

> ### Acts 9:5-6
> *And he said, Who art thou, Lord? And the Lord said, I am Jesus whom thou persecutest: it is hard for thee to kick against the pricks. ⁶And he trembling and astonished said, Lord, what wilt thou have me to do? And the Lord said unto him, Arise, and go into the city, and it shall be told thee what thou must do.*

Notice that, both at Pentecost and on the Damascus Road, this penetrating condemnation brought the same question from the heart of those convicted: "What must I do?" The reason this is true is because a person who is truly repenting will **possess a "godly sorrow"** for the wrong they've done.

Writing to the church at Corinth, Paul drew a clear distinction between two kinds of sorrow. He mentioned "godly sorrow" and "the sorrow of the world."

2 Corinthians 7:9-10

Now I rejoice, not that ye were made sorry, but that ye sorrowed to repentance: for ye were made sorry after a godly manner, that ye might receive damage by us in nothing. [10]For godly sorrow worketh repentance to salvation not to be repented of: but the sorrow of the world worketh death.

The phrase "godly sorrow" could more accurately be translated from the original Greek as "sorrow according to God." Dr. Albert Barnes, in his Notes on the New Testament, says this means, "Such sorrow as shall ... arise from a view of the evil of sin as committed against a holy God."[9] In light of that, one can surmise that "the sorrow of the world" would be any OTHER kind of sorrow a person might feel (such as being sorry you got caught).

What we should recognize in this is that it cannot be something we do halfheartedly. Rather, it involves "all the heart," as is born out in a number of biblical verses.

Joel 2:12

Therefore also now, saith the LORD, turn ye even to me with all your heart, and with fasting, and with weeping, and with mourning:

---

[9]BARNES, A., MURPHY, J. G., COOK, F. C., PUSEY, E. B., LEUPOLD, H. C., & FREW, R. (1996). *Barnes' Notes.* Grand Rapids, Michigan: Baker.

Deuteronomy 4:29

But if from thence thou shalt seek the LORD thy God, thou shalt find him, if thou seek him with all thy heart and with all thy soul.

Jeremiah 29:13

And ye shall seek me, and find me, when ye shall search for me with all your heart.

A godly sorrow, then, is the natural response to seeing sin as God sees it. This perspective will cause us to seek after God with our whole heart. Based on the following verses, it should also involve brokenness and contrition (which is usually evidenced by weeping).

Psalm 34:18

The LORD is nigh unto them that are of a broken heart; and saveth such as be of a contrite spirit.

Psalm 51:17

The sacrifices of God are a broken spirit: a broken and a contrite heart, O God, thou wilt not despise.

In order to truly seek God with all our heart, we need to **make confession to God.** This is borne out in both the Old and New Testaments.

Proverbs 28:13

He that covereth his sins shall not prosper: but whoso confesseth and forsaketh them shall have mercy.

1 John 1:9

If we confess our sins, he is faithful and just to forgive us our sins, and to cleanse us from all unrighteousness.

For some, this might raise the question, "To whom do we confess?" The answer is simple: When your sin is only against God, you only have to confess to Him. There is absolutely no biblical basis for requiring people to make confession to a priest. There may be times we need to confess to someone we have wronged in order to make things right with them, but the practice of confessing our sins to a priest does not have its origins in Scripture.

As we begin to realize the pitiful condition of our souls, we are also made aware of our personal helplessness to correct it. When this happens, it will cause us to **plead for mercy.**

Psalm 51:1

Have mercy upon me, O God, according to thy lovingkindness: according unto the multitude of thy tender mercies blot out my transgressions.

Luke 18:13

And the publican, standing afar off, would not lift up so much as his eyes unto heaven, but smote upon his breast, saying, God be merciful to me a sinner.

Although it may require humility in order for us to do this, there is no question it is good for us to admit our condition and desperate NEED of God! As we do, we should then **ask for forgiveness.**

Hosea 14:2

Take with you words, and turn to the LORD: say unto him, Take away all iniquity, and receive us graciously: so will we render the calves of our lips.

In what is called the Lord's Prayer, Jesus instructed us on the proper method to use when we pray. As part of a proper prayer, we need to ask for forgiveness.

Luke 11:4

And forgive us our sins; for we also forgive every one that is indebted to us. And lead us not into temptation; but deliver us from evil.

Of course, it would do no good to ask for forgiveness while, at the same time, knowing full well we are going to go back and repeat the same sins. Instead, we must **determine to turn from sin with the help of God.**

Ezekiel 18:31

Cast away from you all your transgressions, whereby ye have transgressed; and make you a new heart and a new spirit: for why will ye die, O house of Israel?

Once again, I want you to understand that even though this is an Old Testament Scripture, it is not just something that was required in ancient times. We find in the New Testament that Jesus Himself commanded this.

John 8:11

She said, No man, Lord. And Jesus said unto her, Neither do I condemn thee: go, and sin no more.

You see, biblically, repentance is a type of death. Paul made this abundantly clear.

Romans 6:6

Knowing this, that our old man is crucified with him, that the body of sin might be destroyed, that henceforth we should not serve sin.

When we repent, we become "dead to sin." We crucify the desires of the flesh so we can seek to please God.

Romans 6:1-2

What shall we say then? Shall we continue in sin, that grace may abound? [2]God forbid. How shall we, that are dead to sin, live any longer therein?

Mark 8:34

And when he had called the people unto him with his disciples also, he said unto them, Whosoever will come after me, let him deny himself, and take up his cross, and follow me.

Please understand, while confession is necessary, it is not the ONLY thing the scriptures require in order for us to obtain mercy. We must confess AND forsake our sin.

Proverbs 28:13

He that covereth his sins shall not prosper: but whoso confesseth and forsaketh them shall have mercy.

There is no question anyone can come to Jesus, regardless of their condition. He loves us enough to take us as we are. By the same token, however, He loves us too much to LEAVE us as we are. Remember, Christ came to save us FROM sin, not IN sin!

Matthew 1:21

And she shall bring forth a son, and thou shalt call his name JESUS: for he shall save his people from their sins.

In order to forsake sin, you must literally turn away from it. That will result in a change in our lifestyle. We will now begin to do those things God expects of us.

Luke 6:46

And why call ye me, Lord, Lord, and do not the things which I say?

Having confessed (and determined to forsake) our sins, we

should then accept God's forgiveness. While this may seem to be an unnecessary point, there are untold numbers of individuals who have a difficult time believing God has forgiven them.

Psalm 86:5

For thou, Lord, art good, and ready to forgive; and plenteous in mercy unto all them that call upon thee.

Forgiveness is PROMISED. Therefore, we should BELIEVE God will do it.

1 John 1:9

If we confess our sins, he is faithful and just to forgive us our sins, and to cleanse us from all unrighteousness.

Acts 3:19

Repent ye therefore, and be converted, that your sins may be blotted out, when the times of refreshing shall come from the presence of the Lord;

Isaiah 1:18

Come now, and let us reason together, saith the LORD: though your sins be as scarlet, they shall be as white as snow; though they be red like crimson, they shall be as wool.

Before closing this chapter, I think it would be good to point out what happens when someone has truly repented. Doing so might help a person know when they have truly made things right with God.

First, you will no doubt **experience great joy.** Heaven is rejoicing, and so should you!

Luke 15:7

I say unto you, that likewise joy shall be in heaven over one sinner that repenteth, more than

> *over ninety and nine just persons, which need no*
> *repentance.*

One reason you should feel joy is because you realize the load of sin has been removed. You are no longer under the threat of death!

1 John 1:7

> *But if we walk in the light, as he is in the light, we have fellowship one with another, and the blood of Jesus Christ his Son cleanseth us from all sin.*

Psalm 103:12

> *As far as the east is from the west, so far hath he removed our transgressions from us.*

As a bit of a side note, let me point out something about that last Scripture. Notice that the Psalmist did not say, "As far as the north is from the south," but rather, "as far as the east is from the west." I believe there is a reason for this.

If you were to go to a globe, put your finger anywhere on that sphere, and begin moving it to the north, you will eventually arrive at what we call "the North Pole." At that point, the first movement – regardless of which side of the globe you are on – will ALWAYS be south! When at the North Pole, no matter which way you are facing, your first step can ONLY be southward. The same principle applies when your finger arrives at the South Pole, except the first movement can only be northward.

With this in mind, we come to understand there are two places on Earth where "north" and "south" meet. They come together at the poles.

If, on the other hand, you put your finger on the Equator of that globe, and start moving it eastward, you will begin to realize an important fact. No matter how long you travel to the east, you will NEVER suddenly start going west. If you start moving to the west, there is no point on the globe where you will begin to go east. There is no "East Pole" or "West Pole." Although north and south meet in two different places, east and west NEVER meet!

I believe that is why God tells us that He puts our sins "as far as the east is from the west" and NOT "as far as the north is from the south." Had He used the latter phrase, there would have been reason to believe we will eventually encounter our past transgressions. Since He used the former, however, we can rest assured that we will NEVER see those sins again!

The second thing that will happen when you have truly repented is **you will experience a change of nature.** The sinful things you once loved, you will now hate; the spiritual things you once hated, you will now love.

Ephesians 4:22-24

That ye put off concerning the former conversation the old man, which is corrupt according to the deceitful lusts; 23And be renewed in the spirit of your mind; 24And that ye put on the new man, which after God is created in righteousness and true holiness.

Colossians 3:9-10

Lie not one to another, seeing that ye have put off the old man with his deeds; 10And have put on the new man, which is renewed in knowledge after the image of him that created him:

Earlier in this chapter, I pointed out that John the Baptist preached repentance. In doing so, he also made it clear that true repentance would bear fruit.

Matthew 3:8

Bring forth therefore fruits meet for repentance:

Paul also preached repentance. He said it should manifest

itself in good works.

Acts 26:20

But shewed first unto them of Damascus, and at Jerusalem, and throughout all the coasts of Judaea, and then to the Gentiles, that they should repent and turn to God, and do works meet for repentance.

In conclusion, it is important that I make sure you understand repentance is NOT salvation. Even though you have gone through the process described in this chapter, you cannot yet claim to be "saved." You have only begun the process of salvation. There is more for you to do.

Do not forget the instructions Jesus gave to His disciples before His ascension. He instructed them to preach THREE things – and the process of salvation is not complete until all three have been completed in your life.

Luke 24:46-49

And said unto them, Thus it is written, and thus it behoved Christ to suffer, and to rise from the dead the third day: [47]And that repentance and remission of sins should be preached in his name among all nations, beginning at Jerusalem. [48]And ye are witnesses of these things. [49]And, behold, I send the promise of my Father upon you: but tarry ye in the city of Jerusalem, until ye be endued with power from on high.

Those three things are: (1) repentance; (2) remission of sins in Jesus' name; and (3) the promise of the Father. Thus, repentance is only the FIRST step. We will discuss the next step (remission of sins in Jesus' name) in the next chapter.

CHAPTER 5

THE DOCTRINE OF BAPTISM

PART 1: THE MANDATE

Hebrews 6:1-3

> *Therefore leaving the principles of the doctrine of Christ, let us go on unto perfection; not laying again the foundation of repentance from dead works, and of faith toward God, ²Of the doctrine of baptisms, and of laying on of hands, and of resurrection of the dead, and of eternal judgment. ³And this will we do, if God permit.*

According to the Book of Hebrews, there is a "doctrine" concerning baptisms.[10] The implication, of course, is that there is only one TRUE doctrine (hence the definite article "the") concerning this subject. Furthermore, that doctrine is a part of our very foundation!

As I have already mentioned, the foundation is perhaps the most important structure of any building. Regardless of how beautiful the edifice may be, if the foundation is bad, the building is worthless.

The same may be said about our spiritual foundation. It is absolutely imperative that that our foundation is correct. No part of the foundation can be faulty, because it is only as strong as its

---

[10] While the Scripture refers to plural "baptisms," this chapter will focus on only one baptism – baptism in water. Acts 1:5 also mentions being baptized with the Holy Ghost. That will be dealt with in the next chapter.

weakest point.

Inasmuch as the doctrine of baptism is a part of our foundation, we should readily recognize that this is NOT an area that can be left for "private interpretation." In fact, NO Biblical doctrine can be taken that way!

> **2 Peter 1:20**
> *Knowing this first, that no prophecy of the scripture is of any private interpretation.*

When dealing with any subject, we have an obligation to find out what God's Word says about it. We must then adjust our beliefs accordingly.

In previous chapters, we have discovered the following facts: (1) We must never let tradition supersede truth; (2) Truth is based SOLELY on what the Word of God teaches; and (3) Truth is further determined by comparing our teaching with those of the original Apostles. With those principles in mind, let us consider what the Bible teaches concerning the doctrine of baptism, making sure our viewpoint aligns with that of the Apostles.

In dealing with this subject, the first question we should seek to answer must be the necessity of water baptism. Does God require that we partake of this ordinance, or is it merely "an outward sign of an inward grace"?

To find the correct answers, let us first consider the words of Jesus Himself. No one can argue that what He says is true.

> **John 3:1-5**
> *There was a man of the Pharisees, named Nicodemus, a ruler of the Jews: ²The same came to Jesus by night, and said unto him, Rabbi, we know that thou art a teacher come from God: for no man can do these miracles that thou doest, except God be with him. ³Jesus answered and said unto him, Verily, verily, I say unto thee,*

> *Except a man be born again, he cannot see the*
> *kingdom of God. 4Nicodemus saith unto him,*
> *How can a man be born when he is old? can he*
> *enter the second time into his mother's womb,*
> *and be born? 5Jesus answered, Verily, verily, I*
> *say unto thee, Except a man be born of water and*
> *of the Spirit, he cannot enter into the kingdom of*
> *God.*

Please notice the fact that, in both verse 3 and verse 5, Jesus uses the word "except" (i.e., "except a man be ... he cannot"). The word "except" carries extreme significance, particularly in our text. It is generally defined in the following ways: "With the exclusion of; other than; if it were not for the fact that." Obviously, it signifies that there is an exclusion to the rule which applies to all others outside the "exception."

In verses 3 and 5, Jesus gave a rule, and then provided an exception. Let us, then, consider again what He said.

John 3:3

> *Jesus answered and said unto him, Verily,*
> *verily, I say unto thee, Except a man be born*
> *again, he cannot see the kingdom of God.*

The rule in verse three is: "a man ... cannot see the kingdom of God." The exception was that IF that man is "born again," then the rule does not apply to him.

The problem we now have is verse 3 does not explain what being "born again" means. Inasmuch as this was the first time this phrase had ever been used, Nicodemus was obviously confused. He knew of only one kind of birth (a natural birth). He tried to reconcile that with being "born again."

John 3:4

> *Nicodemus saith unto him, How can a man be*
> *born when he is old? can he enter the second time*

into his mother's womb, and be born?

Because verse 4 presents the question, we must admit that verse 5 is the answer. Jesus was obviously explaining what being "born again" means. We cannot, then, apply our own interpretation to the term.

Defining the new birth, however, can bring a host of varying ideas. Some say being "born again" means accepting Christ as your personal Savior; others say it simply means "believing on Christ;" still others seem to think it is just a reference to church membership.

These are only a few of the definitions being put forth today. Please understand, while it is possible that everyone may be wrong, it is NOT possible that everyone is right!

As I have stated before, if we want to interpret Scripture, we should always do it with other Scriptures. We cannot simply assign our own definition to the term "born again," especially since Jesus Himself defined it for us!

In His answer, Jesus again stated the rule: "a man ... cannot enter into the kingdom of God." He also stated the exception, giving it a clearer definition.

John 3:5

Jesus answered, Verily, verily, I say unto thee,
Except a man be born of water and of the Spirit,
he cannot enter into the kingdom of God.

We cannot dispute the fact that Jesus explained the new birth as being born of water and born of the Spirit. However, what do those terms mean? Because Jesus did not define them in this passage, there are discrepancies among the definitions being put forth today. In order to find the CORRECT definitions, we will need to go to the Scripture to find out what it means to be born of water and born of Spirit.

Before examining the Scriptural explanation for the term

"born of water," let me first address a common misconception. There are those who argue that Jesus spoke of the natural birth when He said a man must be "born of water." They claim that the "birth of water" is a description of the gushing of amniotic fluid from the mother's body as she gives birth. However, this argument will not "hold water" (pardon the pun) since Jesus made this birth an absolute prerequisite for entering the Kingdom of God.

What would be the purpose behind saying, "Unless you are born naturally and spiritually, you cannot enter Heaven"? EVERY human being is born naturally. There would be absolutely no reason to state something so obvious when listing it among the requirements for salvation.

Besides this, there are two main reasons why I cannot believe the term "born of water" is a reference to the natural birth. The first reason is biological.

In order to fully explain this part of my refutation of this argument, let us examine the natural birth process. Just prior to birth, the amniotic sac (i.e., "the bag of waters") usually ruptures, resulting in a rush of water from the mother's body. If the sac ruptures early in labor, as frequently happens, the birth is termed a "dry birth."

If Jesus was speaking of the mother's water breaking as the child is born, then because multitudes have been born a "dry birth," they would then never have been "born of water." As a result, they would be excluded from God's Kingdom because of something completely beyond their control. Remember, Jesus said the water-birth was essential. Would a just God eternally punish a baby because it was dry-born? No, no, a thousand times, no!

The second reason I reject this notion is scriptural. There is simply no other biblical reference to the natural birth which would connect it to the term "born of water." Inasmuch as the Lord made this a requirement for salvation, it seems evident He would have provided us with at least one other witness in the Bible to be certain we interpreted the phrase properly. Since there is NOT a "second witness," there is absolutely no basis for claiming that being born of water is a reference to the natural birthing process.

In finding the proper meaning of Jesus' mandate in John 3:5, it is imperative that we allow Scripture to interpret Scripture. This we will do.

As we do so, we must remember the new birth (and whatever is involved therein) is the ONLY exception which will allow us to be saved; therefore, it is eternally crucial that we find – and obey – the BIBLICAL definition!

In order to interpret this Scripture through the use of another Scripture, we need to be cognizant of the fact that Jesus said we must be born of water in order to be saved. Therefore, we need to find another Scripture which connects water with salvation. By doing this, we can properly interpret the Lord's words to Nicodemus.

Having said this, let us now consider the words Jesus spoke as recorded in the closing chapter of Mark. Here we will find exactly what we are looking for.

Mark 16:16

He that believeth and is baptized shall be
saved; but he that believeth not shall be damned.

There is no question that, in this verse, Jesus clearly connects water with salvation! Therefore, we can safely conclude that "being born of water" refers to baptism, without which we "cannot enter into the kingdom of God."

Mark 16:16 further proves this point in and of itself. Notice the conjunction "and." Its placement in this sentence shows that BOTH believing AND baptism are necessary in order to be saved.

In order to further help you understand what I mean, let us consider the significance of the word "and" when used in another setting. Let us suppose that a man and his friend go to visit a particular restaurant together. Upon his arrival, they see a sign which says, "He that wears a coat and tie shall be allowed to enter." Let us further suppose that one of the men is wearing a very expensive necktie, but no coat. His friend, on the other hand, is wearing a high-dollar sports coat, but does not have on a tie. Will either of these men be allowed to go into the establishment? Of course not! Because the requirement is both coat AND tie, no man will be permitted entry if he only has one or the other.

The same principle applies to Mark 16:16. Jesus emphatically stated that a man must both believe AND be baptized in order to be saved. Therefore, if someone has done one but neglected the other, it is impossible for him to enter God's kingdom.

Some argue against this interpretation based on the second half of the verse: "but he that believeth not shall be damned." It is their contention that Jesus did not specify baptism when He spoke of damnation. Therefore, they say, Jesus was NOT issuing a requirement for baptism.

Surely we can recognize that the lack of the requirement in the second half of the verse does not negate the clear requirement in the first half! Think again about the restaurant analogy. Suppose the sign said, "He that wears a coat and tie shall be allowed to enter, but he who wears no coat is not welcome." Does the fact that the tie is not mentioned in the second half of the statement do away with what was stated in the first half? Absolutely not! If the sign states that you must wear both a coat and tie, then leaving one or the other out of the rest of the sentence does not take away from the necessity of both coat AND tie!

Perhaps another analogy will help to clarify this even more. If someone came to the first man, wanting to borrow his car, he might tell them, "As long as you put gas in it and wash it, you may drive it." Will washing the car alone allow him to use it? No, he must both wash it AND put fuel in the tank.

Now suppose that the full response was, "As long as you put gas in it and wash it, you may drive it; but if you do not put gas in it, you are not going anywhere!" Does the fact that the owner of the vehicle does not list washing the car in the second half of the statement do away with its presence in the first? No – the fact is, if there is no fuel in it, washing it without filling it up will not get anyone anywhere. There would be no need to wash the car if the fuel gage is on empty. RESTATING both requirements is not essential for KEEPING both requirements in place.

When Jesus said that you must believe AND be baptized in order to be saved, He meant exactly what He said. Although many people seem to think He said, "He that believeth and is saved should probably be baptized," there is no question that is NOT what the Lord had in mind. We should recognize that Mark 16:16 and John 3:5 are companion verses in that: (1) Both of them are the words of Jesus; and (2) Both of them mention baptism as being necessary for salvation.

That Jesus made baptism a prerequisite for salvation is further proved by examining the message His Apostles preached. I want to remind you that He gave the explicit instructions concerning their message, specifically naming three things that were to be included.

Luke 24:47-49

And that repentance and remission of sins should be preached in his name among all nations, beginning at Jerusalem. ⁴⁸And ye are witnesses of these things. ⁴⁹And, behold, I send the promise of my Father upon you: but tarry ye in the city of Jerusalem, until ye be endued with power from on high.

Just prior to His ascension, Jesus told the disciples to preach three things. They were: (1) Repentance; (2) Remission of Sins in Jesus' Name; and (3) The Promise of the Father. There can be no doubt that these men understood full well what Jesus meant by each of these phrases. After all, He had just "opened their understanding."

Luke 24:45

Then opened he their understanding, that they might understand the scriptures,

Inasmuch as we have already dealt with the first requirement (repentance), we are ready now to consider the second one, which is "remission of sins ... in His name." In order to find out exactly how this was applied through the teaching of the Apostles, let us go to the very first time sinners asked about salvation (after the birth of the church on the day of Pentecost).

Acts 2:37

Now when they heard this, they were pricked in their heart, and said unto Peter and to the rest of the Apostles, Men and brethren, what shall we do?

In a previous chapter, I said that there is a "law of first mention" that must be considered when trying to interpret the Scriptures. As I explained then, I simply mean the first time a subject is introduced in the Bible, it should be given a more prominent consideration. In other words, the first time a subject is mentioned, it becomes the standard to which other instances in which that subject appears should be compared.

Because the Day of Pentecost was the "birthday of the church," any examples of people being saved which occur prior to Acts 2 cannot be compared to what it takes for us to be saved today. I am confident that no one would argue whether Moses was "saved." Yet I am also confident that no one who understands the Scriptures would claim that we can be saved by doing the same things Moses did to secure HIS salvation. Moses' salvation was prior to Pentecost. It cannot be compared with the plan of salvation required for those of us who are living AFTER the establishment of the church.

Undeniably, then, Acts 2:37-39 provides us with the "first mention" with regards to the question of instructing the lost concerning salvation within the church age. In these verses we find men who had come to realize their sin and guilt and called on the Apostles to show them the way to salvation. "What shall we do?" was the despairing cry of their convicted hearts.

We must not ignore the fact that at this crucial moment when men were wanting to know God's plan of salvation, Peter did not say, "Accept Christ as your personal Savior, and you shall be saved." He did not say, "Pray the sinner's prayer." He did not say, "Just believe." However, Peter DID give them the response Jesus had instructed him to give.

Acts 2:38

Then Peter said unto them, Repent, and be baptized every one of you in the name of Jesus Christ for the remission of sins, and ye shall receive the gift of the Holy Ghost.

Pay close attention to the words Peter spoke. He told the crowd to "be baptized ... in the name of Jesus Christ for the remission of sins". Can anyone argue that this is not EXACTLY what Jesus had told His disciples to preach in Luke 24:47?

I do not want to complicate this lesson (or this book) by the insertion of too many references to the original languages. However, there is something extremely important about the Greek word Peter used which connected baptism to remission of sins. Our English Bible translates it "for" (e.g., "be baptized ... FOR the remission of sins"). This word is translated from the Greek word "eis," which means "in order to," or "in order to obtain." In light of this fact, the phrase could correctly be translated, "be baptized ... in order to obtain remission of sins." You cannot, therefore, have your sins remitted without baptism.

There are some who would argue against this interpretation of "eis." It is their opinion that "eis" would mean "because of," or "because you have obtained" remission of sins. In other words, they contend that a person is to be baptized because their sins have already been remitted (at repentance). Let us examine, however, another passage of New Testament scripture in which the word "eis" is used exactly the same way in exactly the same phrase as it appears in Acts 2:38.

Matthew 26:28

For this is my blood of the new testament, which is shed for many for the remission of sins.

At the Last Supper, Jesus used the very same words Peter would use in his message on the Day of Pentecost. He said His blood was shed "for the remission of sins." Since the same word is used in the same phrase and in the same way, it is safe to conclude that what it means in one, it must mean in the other as well.

To apply the usage mentioned above, we would end up with a strange result. Consider: "For this is my blood ... which is shed for many *because they have already obtained remission of sins.*" Did Jesus shed His blood because the sins of the world had already been remitted? Nobody who has any idea of the gospel scheme believes this. The very idea is absurd.

It is obvious that Jesus shed His blood in order that the repentant might obtain remission. Thus, the word "eis" MUST be used in this phrase to mean "in order to obtain." With that in mind, we use the same definition when interpreting "eis" in Acts 2:38. When Peter said to be baptized "FOR" the remission of sins, he was clearly saying baptism is the mode through which we obtain remission.

Without controversy, the Apostle Peter preached, believed, and practiced baptism as a salvific essentiality. This is seen when Peter (to whom Jesus gave "the keys of the kingdom" in Matthew

16:19) was leading people to salvation. Whether it was to the Jews (Acts 2), the Samaritans (Acts 8), or the Gentiles (Acts 10), baptism was ALWAYS a vital part of Peter's preaching.

In fact, it would be good to pay special attention to the last example mentioned. In this passage, we find the story of a righteous man named Cornelius. By divine intervention and direction, Peter went to Cornelius' house to proclaim salvation to him.

While Peter was preaching, Cornelius and his household received the Holy Ghost and spoke in tongues (verse 46). Although this was a glorious experience, a close reading of the entire passage shows something extremely important about what took place that day.

Acts 10:44-48

While Peter yet spake these words, the Holy Ghost fell on all them which heard the word. ⁴⁵And they of the circumcision which believed were astonished, as many as came with Peter, because that on the Gentiles also was poured out the gift of the Holy Ghost. ⁴⁶For they heard them speak with tongues, and magnify God. Then answered Peter, ⁴⁷Can any man forbid water, that these should not be baptized, which have received the Holy Ghost as well as we? ⁴⁸And he commanded them to be baptized in the name of the Lord. Then prayed they him to tarry certain days.

Peter did not *suggest* baptism. He did not *encourage* baptism. He COMMANDED baptism! If baptism was not essential, why did Peter *command* them to be baptized when they had already received the Holy Ghost? Evidently, baptism IS essential.

My final piece of evidence concerning Peter's belief that men could not be saved unless they were baptized comes from one of the epistles he wrote. As Peter discussed the way that God delivered Noah, he drew an analogy to New Testament salvation.

1 Peter 3:20-21

Which sometime were disobedient, when once the longsuffering of God waited in the days of Noah, while the ark was a preparing, wherein few, that is, eight souls were saved by water. [21]The like figure whereunto even baptism doth also now save us (not the putting away of the filth of the flesh, but the answer of a good conscience toward God,) by the resurrection of Jesus Christ:

Could he have been more specific? According to Peter, just as Noah and his family were separated from the wicked world by water, it is going to be the waters of baptism which will separate the family of God today!

Peter also stated that baptism does not cleanse the outward man. What it does is cleanse the inner man. That is how we can have "a good conscience toward God."

The idea that baptism is essential to salvation is not some new concept. From the very beginning of the world, God showed through many types and shadows that it played a part in His plan to save mankind.

Remember, the Apostles did not have the New Testament from which to preach. Whatever they preached, they had to use the Old Testament as their basis. (In fact, any doctrine which does not have its roots in the Old Testament should probably be reexamined.) Therefore, God was careful to provide PLENTY of examples as witnesses of the necessity of water baptism.

Let us look at a few instances in the Old Testament where God provided us with a "witness" (i.e., a type or symbol) of the prominence baptism would assume in the message of salvation. I think many people will be surprised at just how frequently it appears.

In Genesis I, we find a world that was "without form, and void." Then, the Spirit moved upon the water. The result was a new and living world. Look at the three elements highlighted: a "dead" (non-living) world, the Spirit, and the water.

The Book of Exodus tells of the Children of Israel in Egyptian bondage. God sent a number of plagues upon Egypt to convince them to let His people go. The final plague was death, which could only be avoided through the shedding of blood. As they fled Egypt, the Israelites' only way of escape was through the Red Sea. After passing through the water, they were free from bondage and began a new life. Here we see blood and/or death, water, and freedom.

While they were in the Wilderness, God instructed them to build a tabernacle. The first piece of furniture one encountered when entering the court of the tabernacle was the Brazen Altar, the place of sacrifice, shedding of blood, and death. Next, the priest had to pass by the Brazen Laver, the place of washing and cleansing. From there, they could enter into the tabernacle proper, in which the Spirit of God dwelt.

Before going to the next example, let me just point out that the laver was NOT optional! The Lord told Moses that if any priest tried to bypass the water, he would die.

Exodus 30:20

When they go into the tabernacle of the congregation, they shall wash with water, that they die not; or when they come near to the altar to minister, to burn offering made by fire unto the LORD:

After wandering in the wilderness for forty years, it was finally time to enter Canaan. God told Joshua the Israelites would not be allowed to enter until they honored the covenant of circumcision, requiring the shedding of blood. Once this was accomplished, the only way to take possession of God's promises was to cross the Jordan River. Once they had gone through the water, they finally arrived in Canaan, also known as the Promised Land.

It should be clear that God was establishing a pattern. In every instance, there was shedding of blood and/or death. There was God's Spirit (or freedom or new life). There was also *water*. The pattern is not – and cannot be – complete without the water.

The real strength of using these types to prove the necessity of baptism is the fact that the gospel message itself fits very beautifully into the same pattern I have just laid out for you. This is based on the way Paul defines the gospel in I Corinthians 15.

1 Corinthians 15:1-4

Moreover, brethren, I declare unto you the gospel which I preached unto you, which also ye have received, and wherein ye stand; [2]By which also ye are saved, if ye keep in memory what I preached unto you, unless ye have believed in vain. [3]For I delivered unto you first of all that which I also received, how that Christ died for our sins according to the scriptures; [4]And that he was buried, and that he rose again the third day according to the scriptures:

Herein is the gospel: It is the death, burial, and resurrection of Jesus Christ. We can easily understand how the gospel fits into this pattern by using Acts 2:38 as the key.

Acts 2:38

Then Peter said unto them, Repent, and be baptized every one of you in the name of Jesus Christ for the remission of sins, and ye shall receive the gift of the Holy Ghost.

Peter said we should repent. This is the death, the altar, the wilderness, the lifeless world.

Then he said to be baptized. Here we see the Red Sea, the Jordan River, the Laver, and, according to Romans 6:4, the burial of Jesus.

Finally, we have the promise of receiving the Holy Ghost. This is a beautiful experience, typified by the new and living world, the freedom from Egyptian bondage, the Land of Promise, the presence of God, and the Lord's resurrection.

Furthermore, I should also point out that when Abraham sent his servant to find a wife for Abraham's son (Isaac), Rebekah was found at the well (Genesis 24). The analogy here, of course, is that the true bride of Christ will be found through the waterway!

Another example is the testing of Gideon's army. The final test was performed at the water (Judges 7). God's army will be determined by the water!

Furthermore, we cannot overlook the fact that Paul taught baptism in the New Testament does for us what circumcision in the Old Testament did for the Children of Israel. According to Genesis 17, circumcision was "a token of the covenant" between God and Abraham, and any male descendant who was not circumcised, was not allowed to inherit the promises given to Abraham.

Genesis 17:14

And the uncircumcised man child whose flesh of his foreskin is not circumcised, that soul shall be cut off from his people; he hath broken my covenant.

Let us move now to the New Testament. Writing to the Colossians, Paul explains how baptism is the token of OUR New Covenant.

Colossians 2:11-12

In whom also ye are circumcised with the circumcision made without hands, in putting off the body of the sins of the flesh by the circumcision of Christ: *12Buried with him in baptism, wherein also ye are risen with him through the faith of the operation of God, who hath raised him from the dead.*

The Apostle taught that we "put off the body of the sins of the flesh" when we are "buried with [Christ] in baptism." Thus, the only way to keep from breaking the New Covenant is to be baptized according to Scripture.

Perhaps the most beautiful type, however, does not come from the Old Testament, but from the New. We find it in the Gospel of John.

Before examining the passage in question, however, let us first establish the fact that Jesus is identified as "the last Adam."

1 Corinthians 15:45

And so it is written, The first man Adam was made a living soul; the last Adam was made a quickening spirit.

With that in mind, let us consider how the first Adam's bride came into existence. Once we have done that, we will compare this to the last Adam.

Genesis 2:21-22

And the LORD God caused a deep sleep to fall upon Adam and he slept: and he took one of his ribs, and closed up the flesh instead thereof; *22And the rib, which the LORD God had taken from man, made he a woman, and brought her unto the man.*

To begin with, the first Adam was put to sleep. While he

slept, his bride was created from what came out of his side.

In the Book of Revelation, the church is called the Bride of Christ (see Revelation 21:9). Now let us see from where the last Adam's bride would come.

John 19:30

When Jesus therefore had received the vinegar, he said, It is finished: and he bowed his head, and gave up the ghost.

This verse says that Jesus "gave up the ghost," or died. Thus, in a sense, He was asleep. (See 1 Thessalonians 4:15-17.) Four verses later, we see something coming from His side.

John 19:34

But one of the soldiers with a spear pierced his side, and forthwith came there out blood and water.

What came from the side of the last Adam while He slept? It was blood AND water! From where should the bride of Christ come? According to the analogy, from His side. We are made His bride, therefore, not only through His blood, but we cannot exclude the water that came out simultaneously.

There is a definite connection throughout the Word of God that shows repeatedly how important water is in God's plan of redemption. No honest heart can deny that.

As final evidence, let us look to John's First Epistle. In one sentence, he wraps up everything I have been saying about the Old Testament types AND the Lord's death on the cross.

1 John 5:8

And there are three that bear witness in earth, the spirit, and the water, and the blood: and these three agree in one.

John said "the Spirit, the WATER, and the blood ... agree in one." It is not a coincidence that he lists three elements. Just as the Old Testament repeatedly showed three elements interconnected in God's method of deliverance (death, water, and new life), AND just as Jesus commanded His disciples to preach three things (repentance, remission of sins in His name, and the promise of the Father), AND just as Peter commanded the crowd to do three things (repent, be baptized in Jesus' name, and receive the Holy Ghost), so John says there are three things which "agree in one" – they work together to save us! It was not just the blood, and not just the blood and the Spirit; this work of regeneration cannot be complete without the water!

Note how exquisitely all of these verses come together! In fact, we can also include John 3:5 as yet another Scripture which solidifies my case. There, Jesus said we must not only be born of the Spirit, but we also must be born of the water! There is, therefore, a Scriptural mandate to be baptized in order to be saved.

Having established the fact that baptism is a part of the new birth and is therefore essential for salvation, let us now consider the way in which it should be performed. The question at hand is: Does it matter if we were immersed or sprinkled? As long as water is involved, should that not suffice? In the next section, we will let the Bible answer the question of the proper method of baptism.

PART 2: THE METHOD

Before getting into the Scriptures which deal with the manner in which we should be baptized, it would be helpful if we first have a clear understanding of what the word "baptize" actually means. This word was translated (or, more accurately, transliterated) from the Greek word "baptizo." The most credible sources agree that the verb "baptizo" in the Greek language never has the meaning of to pour or to sprinkle. Rather, it invariably means to dip. Baptizo means immersion, not sprinkling. In fact, there is a different Greek word altogether which is used in the Bible to express sprinkling. This word is "rhantizo" in Greek. (See

Hebrews 9:13, 11:28, and 12:24, and 1 Peter 1:2.)

Lexicographers universally agree that "baptism" and "immersion" are synonymous. When someone says they were baptized by sprinkling, they are actually saying they were immersed by sprinkling – which is, quite frankly, absurd. To put it simply, it would be like saying, "I took a bath by standing in the shower." Of course, "standing in the shower" is NOT "taking a bath," and neither is "sprinkling" a form of "baptism."

Nevertheless, we do not have to rely solely on definitions from the original language. We have all the proof we need in the Scripture.

On two separate occasions, Paul wrote about baptism. In both cases, he compared it with a burial.

Romans 6:4

Therefore we are buried with him by baptism into death: that like as Christ was raised up from the dead by the glory of the Father, even so we also should walk in newness of life.

Colossians 2:12

Buried with him in baptism, wherein also ye are risen with him through the faith of the operation of God, who hath raised him from the dead.

It is obviously impossible to bury a person by sprinkling (or even pouring) dirt on the head of the corpse. The body has to be submerged, or at least completely enclosed! It is absolutely impossible to portray a burial (as baptism does) through any process other than immersion.

There are a number of instances in the Scriptures where the act of baptism is described. In every case, it was ALWAYS by immersion.

Matthew 3:16

And Jesus, when he was baptized, went up straightway out of the water: and, lo, the heavens were opened unto him, and he saw the Spirit of God descending like a dove, and lighting upon him:

Jesus gave us the primary example of the proper method of baptism. The Bible says He "went up ... out of the water" – a clear indication that He had been immersed.

Acts 8:38-39

And he commanded the chariot to stand still: and they went down both into the water, both Philip and the eunuch; and he baptized him. [39]And when they were come up out of the water, the Spirit of the Lord caught away Philip, that the eunuch saw him no more: and he went on his way rejoicing.

Philip and the Ethiopian eunuch followed that example of immersion. In this passage, we are told that "they went down both into the water" and "they were come up out of the water." The references to going down into the water and coming up out of the water definitely show that the baptisms mentioned were done by immersion.

Not only do we have the Biblical examples presented here, but history also backs this up. The early leaders, reformers, and church fathers spoke plainly and explicitly on the subject of immersion. For the sake of time and space, I shall list but a few.

In his Second Treatise, entitled "The Babylonian Captivity of the Church," Martin Luther wrote, "The second part of baptism is the sign, or sacrament, which is that immersion in water from which it derives its name, for the Greek 'baptizo' means 'I immerse,' and 'baptisma' means, 'immersion.' ... "It is therefore indeed correct to say that baptism is a washing away of sins, but the expression is too mild and weak to bring out the full significance of baptism, which is rather a symbol of death and resurrection. For this reason I would have those who are to be baptized completely immersed in the water, as the word says and as the mystery indicates ... because it would be well to give to a thing so perfect and complete a sign that is also complete and perfect. And this is doubtless the way in which it was instituted by Christ. ... Baptism swallowed up your whole body and gave it forth again."[11]

In his *Notes on the New Testament*, John Wesley addressed the term "buried with him," as it is used in Romans 6:4. He wrote that it is "alluding to the ancient practice of baptizing by immersion."[12]

Adam Clark also addressed Romans 6:4 in his *Commentary on the Bible*. There, he states that Paul alluded to "the mode of administering baptism by immersion, the whole body being put under the water."[13]

John Calvin is generally considered to be the "father" of the Presbyterian and Reformed churches. In spite of his own personal opinion regarding the matter, he wrote, "it is evident that the term baptize means to immerse, and that this was the form used by the primitive Church." He also wrote that the Greek term "means to immerse entirely, and it is certain that the custom of thus entirely immersing was anciently observed in the Church."[14]

---

[11] LUTHER, M., LUTHER, M., HERRMANN, E. H., & ROBINSON, P. W. (2016). *The Babylonian captivity of the Church,* 1520. http://public.eblib.com/choice/publicfullrecord.aspx?p=4745406.

[12] WESLEY, J. (1805). *Notes on the New Testament.*

[13] CLARKE, A., & EARLE, R. (1985). *Adam Clarke's commentary on the Bible.* Grand Rapids, Baker Book House.

[14] CALVIN, J., & ALLEN, J. (1960). *Institutes of the Christian religion.*

Long before either of these men existed, however, a man by the name of Eusebius (who has been recognized as the "father of church history") described the first instance on ecclesiastical record of pouring or sprinkling. According to him, the first person to undergo this practice was that of Novatian (a leader of the Roman church) in the year 251. Eusebius said that he (Novatian) "being supposed at the point of death was baptized by aspersion [sprinkling], in the bed on which he lay; if, indeed, it be proper to say that one like him did receive baptism."[15] It is evident that Eusebius did not believe sprinkling to be a proper method of baptism.

If the writings of these men did not help solidify your belief in the practice of immersion, let us also consider a few more references, both religious and secular.

A Summary of Christian History: "Sprinkling became the general mode of baptism ... after about the ninth century."[16]

Christianity Through the Centuries: "Immersion seems to have been widely practiced during the first century."[17]

Liberty Bible Commentary: "The use of baptized indicates the form of baptism as immersion, of dipping or dunking into water."[18]

Funk and Wagnall's New Standard Encyclopedia: "It is

Philadelphia, Presbyterian board of Christian education.

[15] EUSEBIUS, LAKE, K., OULTON, J. E. L., & LAWLOR, H. J. (1992). *The ecclesiastical history.* Cambridge, Mass, Harvard University Press.

[16] BAKER, R. A., & LANDERS, J. M. (2014). *Summary of Christian History.* B & H Publishing Group.

[17] CAIRNS, E. E. (2009). *Christianity through the centuries: a history of the Christian church.*

[18] FALWELL, J., HINDSON, E. E., & KROLL, W. M. (1983). *Liberty Bible commentary.* Lynchburg, Va, Old-Time Gospel Hour.

indisputable that at a very early period the ordinary mode of baptism was by immersion."[19]

The American Peoples Encyclopedia: "In the manner of baptism there is little doubt that the original practice was immersion."[20]

The National Encyclopedia of Reference: "In the primitive church the person to be baptized was dipped."[21]

The World Book Encyclopedia: "In early times, baptism was by complete immersion."[22]

Vine's Expository Dictionary of New Testament Words: "Baptism, consisting of the processes of immersion, submersion, and emergence (from bapto, 'to dip')."[23]

Is there any reason to go on? It would be my hope that, by now, you have read enough to understand that Biblical baptism can ONLY be administered through the process of immersion.

PART 3: THE MODE

In order to help explain the significance of the subject I am about

---

[19] BRAM, L. L. (1996). *Funk & Wagnalls new encyclopedia.* [New York], Funk & Wagnalls.

[20] (1972). *The American peoples encyclopedia 1972.* 1972. New York, Grolier.

[21] ANNANDALE, C., FUREY, F. T., & BLUMENTHAL, W. H. (1915). *The National encyclopedia of reference;* authoritative, practical, complete; an American library embracing science, sociology, philosophy, history, fine arts, languages, religion, law, literature, useful arts, and the many thousands of subjects into which they branch. New York, Standard Bookbinding Co.

[22] WORLD BOOK, INC. (2019). *The world book encyclopedia.*

[23] VINE, W. E., KOHLENBERGER, J. R., SWANSON, J. A., & VINE, W. E. (1984). *The expanded Vine's expository dictionary of New Testament words.* Minneapolis, Minn, Bethany House Publishers.

to address, I ask you to first consider the importance of formulas with regards to chemicals. In chemistry, an improper formula can cause disaster.

For example, if you take one part oxygen, and mix it with two parts hydrogen, the result is H_2O or water. However, if you take that same chemical combination and add one part carbon, the result is CH_2O or Formaldehyde! Remove the hydrogen completely, and you end up with CO – carbon monoxide! Thus, the formula which is used to create a substance (or set of molecules) can make a deadly difference!

I am not a chemist (obviously), and am not simply trying to explain molecular structure. My point in using the example above is to draw a simple analogy. Inasmuch as it is extremely important what formula you use when you are preparing chemicals, does not it make sense that it is even MORE important what formula you use when you are preparing your soul?

We have already discussed the essentiality of water baptism. Since baptism is so important, we must be certain that we use the proper formula when we are baptized.

Acts 19:1-6

And it came to pass, that, while Apollos was at Corinth, Paul having passed through the upper coasts came to Ephesus: and finding certain disciples, ²He said unto them, Have ye received the Holy Ghost since ye believed? And they said unto him, We have not so much as heard whether there be any Holy Ghost. ³And he said unto them, Unto what then were ye baptized? And they said, Unto John's baptism. ⁴Then said Paul, John verily baptized with the baptism of repentance, saying unto the people, that they should believe on him which should come after him, that is, on Christ Jesus. ⁵When they heard this, they were

> *baptized in the name of the Lord Jesus. ⁶And*
> *when Paul had laid his hands upon them, the*
> *Holy Ghost came on them; and they spake with*
> *tongues, and prophesied.*

Consider this: if you had been baptized by John the Baptist, wouldn't you feel pretty secure about your baptism? I think I would! After all, Jesus certainly could not have spoken more highly of John.

Luke 7:28

> *For I say unto you, Among those that are born*
> *of women there is not a greater prophet than John*
> *the Baptist: but he that is least in the kingdom of*
> *God is greater than he.*

The Lord clearly said there was no man born who was greater than John. Yet Paul required these believers who were disciples of John to be re-baptized! There was obviously a very important reason why Paul would do this, and we will discover Paul's reasoning momentarily. Suffice it to say at this point, however, that the simple fact that a person has been baptized does NOT necessarily mean their baptism is adequate!

As I said earlier, the "formula" must be correct. Let us, then, discover God's baptismal formula as stated in the Scriptures.

I know of no better place to begin this discussion than with the words of Jesus Himself. In what is known as "the Great Commission," the Savior instructed His followers concerning this subject.

Matthew 28:19

> *Go ye therefore, and teach all nations,*
> *baptizing them in the name of the Father, and of*
> *the Son, and of the Holy Ghost:*

In order to properly understand this passage, we need to examine its context. This should be readily recognizable by the fact that this verse begins with the word "therefore." This word requires us to find out the reason a person is saying what he is saying. In other words, any time we read the word "therefore," we should do our best to find out what it is there for.

Matthew 28:18

And Jesus came and spake unto them, saying,
All power is given unto me in heaven and in earth.

Before telling His disciples how to baptize, Jesus first informed them that HE had ALL power. Thus, it would be proper to interpret verse 19 as saying, "Because I am the One Who has ALL power, go and do what I am about to tell you."

How much sense does it make to say, "I have all power, so you should baptize in my name as well as two other names?" Let me answer my own question: NONE WHATSOEVER!

What, then, WAS Christ saying? First of all, notice the fact that He said, "Baptizing them in the *name*," and NOT "in the titles." "Father" is NOT a name; it is a title. "Son" is NOT a name; it is a title. "Holy Ghost" is NOT a name; it is a descriptive title.

I am a father, but that is not my name. I am a son, but that is not my name. I am a pastor, a brother, an uncle, a missionary – but none of those titles are my name! Although they describe WHAT I am, they do not identify WHO I am. Only my name can do that.

Jesus specifically said baptism was to take place "in the NAME." Thus, we need to determine what that name is.

Second, notice that He said, "in the name" (singular), not "names" (plural). There is only one name which belongs to the Father, the Son, and the Holy Ghost. That is why He said, "in the name OF the Father, and OF the Son, and OF the Holy Ghost." He was using the "genitive" (or possessive) case and was, therefore, speaking of the name WHICH BELONGS TO the Father, the Son, and the Holy Ghost.

You see, there is a vast difference between "the name Father" and "the name OF the Father." This is best illustrated in the genealogies of Luke 3. Consider, for example, Luke 3:34, where the genitive case is again used, speaking of the son which belonged to a particular father.

Luke 3:34

Which was the son of Jacob, which was the son of Isaac, which was the son of Abraham, which was the son of Thara, which was the son of Nachor,

One example from this verse would be where Luke spoke of Isaac as the "son OF Abraham." If the genitive case was ignored, the result would be "the son Abraham," which would refer to Abraham as being the son mentioned here. However, the scripture was not referring to "the son Abraham", but the son OF Abraham" (which was Isaac).

Just as there is a difference between "the son Abraham," and "the son OF Abraham," so there is a difference between "the name Father" and the "name OF the Father." The Father has a name which must be used. Because of the genitive case, one might well translate this verse to read, "baptizing them in the name which belongs to the Father, and which belongs to the Son, and which belongs to the Holy Ghost."

Interestingly, one well-known televangelist came out with an article several years ago in which he dealt with the subject of water baptism. In the article, he claimed that Father, Son, and Holy Ghost, were, in fact, names.[24] As ridiculous as this claim is, even if it were true, it would still not prove that Jesus was directing the usage of the "three-fold name" (as the televangelist called it) in baptism. Jesus plainly said to baptize "in the name OF the Father, and OF the Son, and OF the Holy Ghost." In other words, Jesus

---

[24] SWAGGART, J. (1982). *The error of the Jesus only doctrine.* [Baton Rouge, La.], [Jimmy Swaggart Ministries].

commanded His followers to baptize "in the Father's name, in the Son's name, and in the Holy Ghost's name." He made it very clear that the Father, Son, and Holy Ghost have A NAME in which we must baptize.

Once again, I assure you it is imperative that we find out what that singular name is. The Bible is very clear about it, if we will simply take the time to search the Scriptures for the answer.

Let us begin by learning the name of the Father. Although some insist the Father's name is "Jehovah" or "Elohim," Jesus gave us a different answer altogether.

John 5:43

I am come in my Father's name, and ye receive me not: if another shall come in his own name, him ye will receive.

Jesus said He came "in His Father's name." Since that is the case, whatever name He came in MUST be the name of His Father as well. Obviously, He came in the name of "Jesus" – that, then, MUST be the Father's name!

The name of the Son should be obvious. Nevertheless, it never hurts to provide Scriptural proof.

Matthew 1:21

And she shall bring forth a son, and thou shalt call his name JESUS: for he shall save his people from their sins.

The angel specifically told Joseph what the name of the Son would be. His name was Jesus.

What, then, is "the name of the Holy Ghost"? Again, there is no need for speculation. Jesus told us what it is.

John 14:26

But the Comforter, which is the Holy Ghost, whom the Father will send in my name, he shall

> *teach you all things, and bring all things to your*
> *remembrance, whatsoever I have said unto you.*

The Comforter (which is the Holy Ghost) was sent in the same name in which the Son came. Therefore, the name of the Holy Ghost is Jesus!

It is really not that complicated. Paul explained this beautiful truth when he wrote to the church of Ephesus.

Ephesians 3:15
> *Of whom the whole family in heaven and earth*
> *is named,*

Paul said the "whole family" shares the same name! What name is that? Well, Peter stated that there is "none other name" than the name of Jesus!

Acts 4:12
> *Neither is there salvation in any other: for*
> *there is none other name under heaven given*
> *among men, whereby we must be saved.*

The only way a person can truly obey Matthew 28:19 is if they baptize using the singular NAME (not titles) which belongs to the Father, Son, and Holy Ghost – and that name is Jesus!

There is no name higher than the name of Jesus. It is above every name!

Philippians 2:9-11
> *Wherefore God also hath highly exalted him,*
> *and given him a name which is above every*
> *name: [10]That at the name of Jesus every knee*
> *should bow, of things in heaven, and things in*
> *earth, and things under the earth; [11]And that*
> *every tongue should confess that Jesus Christ is*
> *Lord, to the glory of God the Father.*

As has already been pointed out, we should always strive to

find more than one "witness" for any doctrine to which we adhere. If we cannot find another verse of Scripture to back up our interpretation of a particular verse or passage, then our interpretation is most likely wrong.

Do not misunderstand me. I am not saying the Scripture is wrong. I am saying our interpretation of the Scripture is wrong.

I have taught doctrinal seminars in many places, both across the United States and overseas. Everywhere I go, I ask the attendees to provide for me one or two additional witnesses in the Bible showing where Jesus intended for us to use the words "Father, Son, and Holy Ghost" as the proper formula for baptism. I have yet to be given even ONE. The simple fact of the matter is nowhere in the New Testament can you find ONE example of ANYONE being baptized using the triune formula. It is *always* done in the name of Jesus!

While I have not been able to get one witness to prove that Matthew 28:19 means we should use the "three-fold name," I AM able to produce a NUMBER of witnesses proving baptism should be done in the name of Jesus Christ. Let us consider those witnesses now.

Acts 2:38

Then Peter said unto them, Repent, and be baptized every one of you in the name of Jesus Christ for the remission of sins, and ye shall receive the gift of the Holy Ghost.

Acts 8:16

(For as yet he was fallen upon none of them: only they were baptized in the name of the Lord Jesus.)

Acts 10:48

And he commanded them to be baptized in the name of the Lord. Then prayed they him to tarry certain days.

Acts 19:5

When they heard this, they were baptized in the name of the Lord Jesus.

Acts 22:16

And now why tarriest thou? arise, and be baptized, and wash away thy sins, calling on the name of the Lord.

Here are not two, not three, but FIVE witnesses attesting to the fact that the singular name was exclusively used in baptism. The law only required "two or three," but we have FIVE! That ought to be enough. However, we are not finished.

1 Corinthians 1:13

Is Christ divided? was Paul crucified for you?
or were ye baptized in the name of Paul?

Paul indicated that the Corinthians had been baptized in the name of the ONE Who was crucified. Who is that One? Obviously, they had been baptized in the name of Jesus!

That, then, makes SIX witnesses to the fact that the proper interpretation of Matthew 28:19 requires use of the name of Jesus. However, we are STILL not finished!

Colossians 3:17

And whatsoever ye do in word or deed, do all
in the name of the Lord Jesus, giving thanks to
God and the Father by him.

In teaching doctrinal seminars in Africa, I often ask the pastors a series of questions. I will generally pick one out of the crowd, have him stand, and then ask, "Do you believe that God answers prayer?" When he responds positively, I ask, "Do you conclude your prayers by saying, 'In the name of the Father, and of the Son, and of the Holy Ghost, Amen'"? He invariably responds, "No! I say, 'In the name of Jesus!'" When I ask why, I am usually told something to the effect of, "Because there is power in the name of Jesus!"

I then ask, "Do you believe in praying for the sick?" Again I will get an answer in the affirmative. I then ask, "Do you lay hands on them and say, 'In the name of the Father, and of the Son, and of the Holy Ghost, be healed'?" When he tells me he doesn't, I ask what he DOES say. His response will generally be, "I say, 'In Jesus' name!'" Why? Again, he explains, "Because there's power in the name of Jesus."

I will then ask a third question: "Do you believe in casting out devils?" The answers and follow-up questions continue in the same pattern I have already described. That, too, is done "In the name of Jesus" because "there's power in that name!"

My final question is, "If you pray in Jesus' name, heal the sick in Jesus' name, and cast out devils in Jesus' name, why do you not baptize in Jesus' name? If that is where the power is, that is the name you should use in baptism! After all, Paul said, 'Do ALL in the name of the Lord Jesus' – not just prayer, healing, and casting out devils – ALL – and that includes water baptism!"

Thus, I have now provided seven (considered by many to be God's number of perfection or completion) witnesses that proper obedience to Matthew 28:19 can ONLY be through the use of the name above every name. The name of the Father, Son, and Holy Ghost IS the name of Jesus!

In response to the above-mentioned discussion, I am often asked, "If it all means the same thing, isn't using the triune formula acceptable?" My response is an emphatic, "NO!"

It is important to recognize that there is a vast difference between obedience and repetition. To repeat someone's words is NOT the same as obedience to those words. For example, if someone said to me, "Please close the door," and I turned to someone else and said, "Please close the door," I would NOT have obeyed the command. I would have simply repeated it.

Jesus did NOT say, "Repeat these words: I baptize you in the name of the Father, and of the Son, and of the Holy Ghost." Rather, He expects us to obey the command to baptize IN THE NAME which belongs to the Father, Son, and Holy Ghost. That name, as we have shown, is Jesus.

Throughout this book, we have pointed out the instructions that Jesus gave to His followers. He said that "repentance and remission of sins would be preached *in His name* ... beginning at Jerusalem."

> ### Luke 24:47
> *And that repentance and remission of sins should be preached in his name among all nations, beginning at Jerusalem.*

I have also pointed out how this is exactly what happened. On the Day of Pentecost, Peter preached to the convicted crowd in Jerusalem, telling them to "repent, and be baptized ... in the name of Jesus Christ." Thus, remission of sins WAS preached "in His name ... beginning at Jerusalem."

To insist that we should use the titles when baptizing is to say the disciples were wrong in the way they practiced this sacrament. Does anyone really believe that Peter (and the rest of the disciples as well) misunderstood the Lord's command as recorded in Matthew 28:19?

I have actually heard people say, "I would rather obey Jesus than Peter," as though the two contradicted one another. While this is a VERY common argument, people do not understand the magnitude of their dispute. When you obey what Peter said, you ARE obeying Jesus!

Consider Acts 1:13. According to this verse, Matthew was present at Pentecost when Peter said what he did.

Acts 1:13

And when they were come in, they went up into an upper room, where abode both Peter, and James, and John, and Andrew, Philip, and Thomas, Bartholomew, and Matthew, James the son of Alphaeus, and Simon Zelotes, and Judas the brother of James.

Why did Matthew not correct Peter and remind him of what Jesus really said? If Peter contradicted Jesus, it seems to me Matthew should have run to him and exclaimed, "Wait, Peter! That is NOT what Jesus said!" Yet the Bible records no words of dissention from the one who penned Matthew 28:19. In fact, not only did Matthew not correct Peter, but according to Acts 2:14, Matthew stood up in agreement with Peter!

Acts 2:14

But Peter, standing up with the eleven, lifted up his voice, and said unto them, Ye men of Judaea, and all ye that dwell at Jerusalem, be this known unto you, and hearken to my words:

There is a clear reason behind Matthew's actions. He knew Peter was explaining and fulfilling what Jesus had said, not contradicting or destroying it.

Will anyone dare say that the Apostles gave wrong instructions to more than 3,000 hungry souls on the day of Pentecost? Consider what this would imply! It would imply: (1) the inspiration imparted to the Apostles was useless, since they ignored what Jesus had told them to do; (2) Christ's personal instruction for more than three years (not to mention the final teachings for 40 days after His resurrection) was wasted, since they *still* disobeyed His commands; (3) the plain statement in Luke 24:45 that the Lord Himself "opened their understanding" was a lie, inasmuch as they did NOT understand; and (4) the anointing of the Holy Ghost at Pentecost was nothing more than a farce, because God would never anoint a lie!

To say, "I would rather obey Jesus than Peter," charges Christ with showing less discernment in the choice of His Apostles than the average business man exhibits in the hiring of his employees. Yet this is the very thing some people have dared to do!

When we look at the words of an inspired Apostle, we cannot summarily reject those words. That is especially true of THIS Apostle (Peter). After all, he was given the "keys of the kingdom," and whatever he "bound on earth" would be "bound in heaven," and whatever he "loosed on earth" would be "loosed in heaven."

Matthew 16:19

And I will give unto thee the keys of the kingdom of heaven: and whatsoever thou shalt bind on earth shall be bound in heaven: and whatsoever thou shalt loose on earth shall be loosed in heaven.

THIS is the one who said to be baptized in Jesus' name! The Lord made it clear that He – and all of Heaven – would stand behind the words spoken by Peter when under the inspiration of the Holy Ghost.

My friend, if you are not willing to trust the words of an inspired Apostle, then you might as well throw away the entire New Testament. Each of these 27 books was written by men under the same inspiration Peter was under when he gave the baptismal formula in Acts 2:38! While you are at it, you might as well throw away the entire Old Testament as well, for it was written in the same fashion!

2 Peter 1:21

For the prophecy came not in old time by the will of man: but holy men of God spake as they were moved by the Holy Ghost.

Do you really think God would allow such an enormous

mistake or contradiction in His word? EVERY ONE of the Apostles baptized according to the formula which is found in Acts 2:38. Surely you do not think ALL the Apostles were wrong and disobeyed Jesus?

Remember that Jesus Himself left no written word. We depend entirely on the word of His Apostles for the only record we have of His commandments. In fact, Jesus said that we would believe on Him THROUGH THE WORD OF HIS APOSTLES!

John 17:20

Neither pray I for these alone, but for them also which shall believe on me through their word;

I spent an entire chapter on this principle. We are "built upon the foundation of the Apostles and prophets."

Ephesians 2:20

And are built upon the foundation of the Apostles and prophets, Jesus Christ himself being the chief corner stone;

Furthermore, Paul repeatedly showed the importance of believing what these men said. For instance, he said that those who are spiritual will recognize the writings of the Apostles as the commandments of the Lord.

1 Corinthians 14:37

If any man think himself to be a prophet, or spiritual, let him acknowledge that the things that I write unto you are the commandments of the Lord.

The Apostle John was just as emphatic. He said that it is the teachings of the Apostles which determine whether we are in truth or error!

1 John 4:6

We are of God: he that knoweth God heareth

us; he that is not of God heareth not us. Hereby
know we the spirit of truth, and the spirit of error.

I feel certain that those who proudly proclaim, "I would rather obey Jesus than Peter," say it sincerely and with good intentions. But good intentions and sincerity cannot be substituted for truth.

Proverbs 14:12

There is a way which seemeth right unto a man,
but the end thereof are the ways of death.

I WOULD TO GOD THAT PEOPLE REALLY WOULD WANT TO OBEY JESUS! If they did, they would be baptized by immersion in Jesus' name!

Baptism could, in one sense, be likened to a check. I could write you a check for a large sum of money and sign it "Father, Son, and Husband," but you would not (could not) receive one cent until I placed my name (i.e., the name of the one providing the remittance) on that check.

The name of the payer MUST be applied before the check is valid. So, in baptism, Jesus Christ has written us "a check" for remission of sins. Until His name is applied, the baptism is not valid. It is WORTHLESS! When you are baptized in the titles "Father, Son, and Holy Ghost," all you get is wet!

Of course, some will argue that Jesus is not "writing a check" for remission of sins through baptism. If so, you obviously did not read the section of this chapter entitled, "The Mandate." There, I showed through Scripture that remission of sins can ONLY come through baptism.

It is important to understand that baptism, like a check, does not supply the promised remittance until the name of the "Payer" is involved. To be blunt, the truth of the matter is if you have not been baptized in the name of Jesus, your sins have never been remitted.

In order to help establish the fact that obedience to Jesus' words in Matthew 28:19 requires obedience to Peter's words in Acts 2:38, et al, let us consider some historical proof. While the Scriptures themselves should be all the proof we need, I will nevertheless provide other documentation as well.

Earlier, I mentioned an article written by a well-known televangelist. In his treatise, he claimed that the use of the Trinitarian baptismal formula is abundantly confirmed by the earliest Christian writings. He went on to say that the Acts 2:38 formula has no historical support at all.[25] Either the author was mistaken, deceived, or untruthful. History is replete with proof that baptism in Jesus' name is the ONLY correct way to baptize.

The Encyclopedia Britannica, "Everywhere in the oldest sources it is stated that baptism took place in the name of Jesus."[26]

The Westminster Dictionary of Church History, "The Trinitarian formula did not emerge until the second century."[27]

The Interpreter's Dictionary of the Bible, "The evidence of Acts 2:38, 10:48 (cf. 8:16, 19:5), supported by Galatians 3:27, and Romans 6:3, suggest that baptism in early Christianity was administered, not in the three-fold name, but in the name of the Lord Jesus."[28]

The New International Standard Bible Encyclopedia, "No record of the Trinitarian formula can be discovered in the Acts of the Apostles. The baptisms recorded in the New Testament after the Day of Pentecost are administered in the name of Jesus Christ. ...

---

[25] SWAGGART, J. (1982). *The error of the Jesus only doctrine.* [Baton Rouge, La.], [Jimmy Swaggart Ministries].

[26] (1974). *Encyclopedia Britannica.* Chicago, Encyclopedia Britannica

[27] BRAUER, J. C., & GERRISH, B. A. (1971). *The Westminster dictionary of church history.* Philadelphia, Westminster Press.

[28] (1982). *The interpreter's dictionary of the Bible* Suppl., Suppl. New York, Abingdon Press.

That this formula was the established usage in the Christian Church is proven by records of baptisms in Justin and Tertullian."[29]

The Dictionary of the New Testament, "It is maintained that the formula at first ran in the name of the Lord Jesus."[30]

Harpers Bible Dictionary, "The Trinitarian formula was a late addition."[31]

Vines Expository Dictionary of New Testament Words, "The phrase ... 'baptizing them into the Name' ... would indicate that the 'baptized' person was closely bound to, or became the property of, the one into whose name he was 'baptized.'"[32]

The Theology of the New Testament, "There is the fact that from the very beginning, baptism undoubtedly was performed in the name of Jesus, i.e., with the pronouncing of the name and hence with the invocation of Jesus."[33]

I am well aware that the things I have stated in this chapter are contrary to common practice today. However, no one can dispute the fact that I have shown you what "thus saith the Word of God" concerning the matter of baptism. It does not matter to God what "the majority" preach or teach. He does not run His Kingdom based on principles of democracy. He does not take a vote and decide what is true based on how many people agree.

---

[29] BROMILEY, G. W. (2009). *The International standard Bible encyclopedia.* Grand Rapids, Mich, W.B. Eerdmans.

[30] LÉON-DUFOUR, X. (1983). *Dictionary of the New Testament.* New York, Harper & Row.

[31] S., M., & MILLER, A. L. (1900). *Harper's Bible Dictionary.*

[32] VINE, W. E., KOHLENBERGER, J. R., SWANSON, J. A., & VINE, W. E. (1984). *The expanded Vine's expository dictionary of New Testament words.* Minneapolis, Minn, Bethany House Publishers.

[33] KÜMMEL, W. G. (1974). *Theology of the New Testament.* [Place of publication not identified], SCM.

The Apostle Paul made this point abundantly clear. He said in no uncertain terms that, if necessary, we should "let God be true, and EVERY man a liar" (Romans 3:4). Rather than trying to base our doctrine on the view of the majority, we must base it SOLELY upon the Word of God! If we do, we will require baptism by immersion in the name of Jesus Christ.

PART 4: QUESTIONS ANSWERED

Before we bring this chapter to an end, let us consider some of the objections which are often asked concerning baptism. Obviously, I do not have the time or space to include EVERY question. Therefore, I will address the more common ones I have encountered either at home or abroad.

1. *"The Thief on the Cross was not Baptized."*

Luke 23:38-43

> *And a superscription also was written over him in letters of Greek, and Latin, and Hebrew, THIS IS THE KING OF THE JEWS. ³⁹And one of the malefactors which were hanged railed on him, saying, If thou be Christ, save thyself and us. ⁴⁰But the other answering rebuked him, saying, Dost not thou fear God, seeing thou art in the same condemnation? ⁴¹And we indeed justly; for we receive the due reward of our deeds: but this man hath done nothing amiss. ⁴²And he said unto Jesus, Lord, remember me when thou comest into thy kingdom. ⁴³And Jesus said unto him, Verily I say unto thee, To day shalt thou be with me in paradise.*

To a great degree, this question was answered indirectly in the opening section of this chapter. There, I dealt with the fact that the church did not begin until Pentecost. Because of this, any reference to being saved that took place prior to Acts 2 cannot be compared to the way people are saved in the church age.

The example I gave at that time was Moses. I believe he was "saved," yet what it took for him to be saved will not get me into the Kingdom of God.

Regardless of whether the reader agrees that the church began at Pentecost, it cannot be denied that the thief did not experience redemption in the way we do. The reason this is undeniable is based on Paul's definition of the gospel.

1 Corinthians 15:1-4

Moreover, brethren, I declare unto you the gospel which I preached unto you, which also ye have received, and wherein ye stand; [2]By which also ye are saved, if ye keep in memory what I preached unto you, unless ye have believed in vain. [3]For I delivered unto you first of all that which I also received, how that Christ died for our sins according to the scriptures; [4]And that he was buried, and that he rose again the third day according to the scriptures:

Herein is the gospel: It is the death, burial, AND resurrection of Jesus Christ – not just His death! Furthermore, Paul not only defined the gospel in the passage cited above, he also explained it is the gospel "by which ... ye are saved." Inasmuch as it happened PRIOR to the burial and resurrection, the gospel plan had not even been completed at the time of the thief's death!

Something else to consider is the fact that both Paul and Peter mentioned our need to "obey the gospel" (see 2 Thessalonians 1:8 and 1 Peter 4:17). How do we "obey" the death, burial, and resurrection of Christ? We do so by experiencing it for ourselves. This is accomplished through obedience to Acts 2:38: We "die" through repentance, are "buried" through baptism in Jesus' name, and are "resurrected" when we receive the gift of the Holy Ghost!

This brings us to another important reason why we cannot compare the thief's salvation to our own. When the thief hung on the cross, the Spirit of God was not yet given because Jesus was not yet glorified.

John 7:39

(But this spake he of the Spirit, which they that believe on him should receive: for the Holy Ghost was not yet given; because that Jesus was not yet glorified.)

Jesus told Nicodemus that entrance into His kingdom was predicated upon a man being "born of water and of the Spirit" (John 3:5). How could the thief have been "born of the Spirit" if the Spirit was not given until Jesus was glorified?

In short, the thief was, indeed, saved. He was NOT saved, however, under the same New Testament requirements which began at Pentecost.

2. *"The Philippian Jailer was Only Told to Believe"*

Acts 16:31

And they said, Believe on the Lord Jesus Christ, and thou shalt be saved, and thy house.

It is very true that Paul answered the jailer, "Believe on the Lord Jesus Christ and thou shalt be saved." However, it is NOT true that "believe on the Lord Jesus" was ALL he said.

One thing to keep in mind in examining this passage was that Paul was the first man to carry the gospel into Philippi. No one there had heard about this great salvation which Jesus could bring.

Like the others in his city, the jailer was someone who could not be made to understand the plan of salvation until he first acknowledged that Christ really was the Messiah. Paul was saying, "If you will believe that Jesus was the Christ, I can explain to you how to be saved." Why tell a man to offer a prayer of repentance to Jesus unless he believes that Jesus is the Christ? The first step in anyone's salvation is to believe. That is NOT, however, the final step.

If Paul meant, as some say, that in the moment the jailer believed he became saved, there is a great problem with the remainder of that verse. Paul said, "Believe on the Lord Jesus Christ and thou shalt be saved AND THINE HOUSE!" If the jailer was immediately saved upon believing, then at the same instant his entire family became saved whether they believed or not!

Paul was not guaranteeing immediate salvation. Rather, he said, "thou SHALT [future tense] be saved." Salvation did not take place until later.

To substantiate this claim, you only need to keep reading. The two verses which follow verse 31 offer the clarity needed for complete understanding.

Acts 16:32-33

And they spake unto him the word of the Lord, and to all that were in his house. ³³And he took them the same hour of the night, and washed their stripes; and was baptized, he and all his, straightway.

As you can see, Paul did not JUST tell him to believe. It was not until AFTER making that statement, the he "spake unto him the word of the Lord." When he did, he MUST have included baptism.

Why else would the jailer risk his life by taking these prisoners out of jail in the middle of the night to perform a religious ceremony? Under the laws of his day, he could have been put to death for such an act. Yet, the jailer did exactly that. It should be easy to see that Paul did, indeed, tell the jailer that baptism was essential.

3. *"We are Saved by Faith and not Works"*

Ephesians 2:8-9

For by grace are ye saved through faith; and
that not of yourselves: it is the gift of God: ⁹Not
of works, lest any man should boast.

This argument is often worded "faith plus nothing, minus nothing." Regardless of the way in which it is presented, the point is that baptism is a "work," and to preach the necessity of baptism is to preach salvation by works.

All of these statements must be closely examined in order to fully understand the fallacious concepts involved. Even though it sounds logical, it is far from Biblical.

Please pay close attention to the wording of Ephesians 2:8-9. We are saved by grace *through* faith. It is neither our works NOR our faith which saves us. It is His grace! Our faith becomes the agent through which grace is made available.

The word "faith" here, however, does not mean simple belief. Rather, it connotes conviction — it is a belief which motivates the believer to action. Without obedience, one does not have biblical faith. If our works do not accompany our faith, then our "faith" is dead.

James 2:17

Even so faith, if it hath not works, is dead,
being alone.

To say that salvation comes by "faith plus nothing, minus nothing" is to utter a clear contradiction of scriptural truth. Not only did James say that a lack of works makes our faith worthless, he goes on to emphatically state that we are justified by our works. He proves this through the examples of Abraham and Rahab.

James 2:23-26

And the scripture was fulfilled which saith,
Abraham believed God, and it was imputed unto
him for righteousness: and he was called the

> *Friend of God. ²⁴Ye see then how that by works a*
> *man is justified, and not by faith only. ²⁵Likewise*
> *also was not Rahab the harlot justified by works,*
> *when she had received the messengers, and had*
> *sent them out another way? ²⁶For as the body*
> *without the spirit is dead, so faith without works*
> *is dead also.*

Did you notice verse 24? James unequivocally stated that we are justified by works "and *not by faith only.*"

If what James wrote is not sufficient evidence, let me provide a second witness. Consider what John the Beloved wrote in his first epistle.

1 John 2:4

> *He that saith, I know him, and keepeth not his*
> *commandments, is a liar, and the truth is not in*
> *him.*

It is simply impossible to be saved by "faith plus nothing, minus nothing!" This is especially true about baptism, since Peter plainly stated that "baptism doth also now save us."

1 Peter 3:21

> *The like figure whereunto even baptism doth*
> *also now save us (not the putting away of the filth*
> *of the flesh, but the answer of a good conscience*
> *toward God,) by the resurrection of Jesus Christ:*

Furthermore, while we are on the subject of justification by works, it is also interesting to note that 1 Corinthians 6:11 teaches that we are justified in Jesus' name. Our works, including water baptism, must be done in His name!

1 Corinthians 6:11

> *And such were some of you: but ye are washed,*
> *but ye are sanctified, but ye are justified in the*

name of the Lord Jesus, and by the Spirit of our
God.

By the way, look again at the two things Paul said brought about washing, sanctification, and justification: the name of Jesus and the Spirit of God. That sounds a lot like John 3:5 – born of water and Spirit! Indeed, it is just another verification that our interpretation of that verse is correct.

4. *"In the Name Of" Actually Means "By the Authority Of."*

Acts 2:38
Then Peter said unto them, Repent, and be
baptized every one of you in the name of Jesus
Christ for the remission of sins, and ye shall
receive the gift of the Holy Ghost.

There are those who argue that the phrase "in the name of" (as used in Acts 2:38) actually means "by the authority of." To further explain this, they will quote the phrase, "Stop in the name of the Law."

I actually heard a man try to explain this interpretation during a debate many years ago. In defending his viewpoint, he referred to the usage of the phrase in the Old Testament story of David sending his men to ask for recompense from Nabal.

1 Samuel 25:5
And David sent out ten young men, and David
said unto the young men, Get you up to Carmel,
and go to Nabal, and greet him in my name:

1 Samuel 25:9
And when David's young men came, they spake
to Nabal according to all those words in the name
of David, and ceased.

After reading these verses, the man insisted that David's servants were not literally SPEAKING David's name. He said they merely went in David's authority.

Much to his dismay, when the time came for his opponent to respond, he did so with joy. He smiled as he read the verse following the one where his opponent had left off.

1 Samuel 25:10

And Nabal answered David's servants, and said, Who is David? and who is the son of Jesse? there be many servants now a days that break away every man from his master.

His reply was that evidently David's servants DID "literally speak the name," inasmuch as Nabal asked them who David was! Nabal would not have known to ask such a question had the servants not verbally mentioned their leader's name!

Of course, trying to insist that "in the name of" means "by the authority of" does not even make grammatical sense when used in verses regarding baptism. Think about it: In Acts 2, Peter was instructing the HEARERS to be baptized "in the name of" Jesus. He was not speaking to the BAPTIZERS, but to those needing baptism. How could one possibly think Peter was telling the crowd that they had to use Jesus' authority in order to GET baptized? Of course, that is not what those who use this argument really mean to imply, but it IS the way it would most accurately be applied were it true.

Furthermore, trying to make the phrase "in the name of" mean "by the authority of" would certainly change the meaning of a number of other verses. One example is found in Mark's gospel.

Mark 13:5-6

And Jesus answering them began to say, Take heed lest any man deceive you: ⁶For many shall come in my name, saying, I am Christ; and shall deceive many.

Let us insert the suggested interpretation into this verse and see what happens. "For many shall come *by my authority* ... and shall deceive many." Surely no one thinks Jesus was saying the deceivers would come by His authority? Of course that is not what He was saying. He did say, however, that they would come *in His name*.

A close look at the original Greek will clear this matter up rather well. In Acts 10:48, for example, "in the name" is "*en to onomati*," which should be literally translated, "with or at the mention of the name." Another example is Acts 2:38, where the actual rendering is "*epi to onomati*," or "when the name is mentioned, using the name." In both instances, the "mention of the name" is implicit in the instruction. I do not deny that authority is involved. I only deny that it can be accessed without the direct, literal invoking of the name through which that authority comes.

5. "What About Those Who Cannot?"

Invariably, every time I teach a doctrinal seminar in Africa, I am asked about those who "cannot" be baptized. The one asking the question will either ask about someone who is incarcerated, or on their death bed, or (in the case of one seminar) in a remote geographical location where baptism would be "impossible." (In that particular case, the individual wanted to know about people who live in places where all the water is perpetually frozen.)

Just as invariably, I will smile and respond – as gently as possible – that the very question itself is suspect. As I look around the room, I tell them, "None of you are in prison. None of you appear to be on your death bed." To the one who asked about frozen lakes, I simply reminded them that they live in Africa, and do not have to worry about such scenarios. I tell them that, at the moment, I am not preaching to people in those conditions, and what will happen to them is totally irrelevant. The important thing is not "what will THEY do," but "what will YOU do?" YOU are the one who has heard the message. YOU are the one who will have to give an answer for what you have clearly seen in the

Scriptures. It is important that we let God sort THEM out, and even MORE important that YOU obey what you have heard!

In spite of that being my first response, I generally deal with the three scenarios mentioned, taking them one at a time. The first one (incarceration) is fairly easy, because in most cases, those in prison CAN be baptized. In the event that they cannot, the answer I give to the third situation will apply to this one as well.

The second condition that is so often mentioned involves those on their deathbeds. Thankfully, I can respond to them with a personal testimony. When I was but a new convert, not yet in my teens, my 77-year old grandmother became deathly ill. The doctors were convinced that she would not live through the night and told my mother that she needed to contact any of the family members who might want to say their goodbyes.

We learned later that, although my grandmother was diagnosed as being comatose, she heard everything that was said that night. She knew she was dying. She also knew she was not ready for eternity. In spite of the fact that she could not speak, she prayed to God in her mind, promising Him that if He would spare her life and let her get out of the hospital, she would go to the church I attended and make things right with the Lord.

God heard her prayer and raised her up. She kept her promise. She went to church, repented of her sins, was baptized in Jesus' name, and was filled with the Holy Ghost. Just a few months later, the Lord took her home to be with Him.

I shared this to illustrate how, if a person is truly sincere and WANTS to obey the Word of God, the Lord Jesus WILL make a way! He is not willing that ANY should perish! (See 2 Peter 3:9.)

That brings me to the final example that is often mentioned – those who are in a geographic location (or other situation) that would seemingly prohibit them from being baptized. In order to answer this question, I take them to a Biblical example.

Acts 8:26

And the angel of the Lord spake unto Philip, saying, Arise, and go toward the south unto the way that goeth down from Jerusalem unto Gaza, which is desert.

First, I like to point out the area involved. According to the Bible, it was a desert – a place where water was scarce at best, and non-existent at worst.

Next, I show them that the individual around whom this incident revolves was from Africa. He was an Ethiopian.

Acts 8:27

And he arose and went: and, behold, a man of Ethiopia, an eunuch of great authority under Candace queen of the Ethiopians, who had the charge of all her treasure, and had come to Jerusalem for to worship,

For the most part, they know the story of how the Ethiopian wanted clarity concerning Isaiah's writings. They know that Philip "joined himself" to the chariot (see Acts 8:29) and "preached unto him Jesus" (Acts 8:35).

Something they fail to recognize, however, is this story is unfolding in a geographical location where baptism would be deemed "impossible." It was not impossible, however, due to something that many seem to just skip over when reading.

Acts 8:36

And as they went on their way, they came unto a certain water: and the eunuch said, See, here is water; what doth hinder me to be baptized?

My question is this: Where did this water come from, since these two men were in the desert? We are not talking about some small puddle, or a drizzling spring. We are talking about enough water that these men "went down both into the water" (Acts 8:38).

This was at the very least a deep pool of water.

I do not know how the water got there. I only know that, when a hungry heart sincerely wanted to be baptized, my God made a way for him to do so!

If God provided a pool in the desert for the Ethiopian, He can make a way in the prison for the inmate, in the hospital room for the dying, and even for the ones in the frozen tundra! His power has not diminished.

Hebrews 13:8

Jesus Christ the same yesterday, and to day, and for ever.

I have enough confidence in the God I serve to believe with all my heart He would never make a command which applies to everyone and yet know there would be situations in which that command could not be fulfilled. If He requires it, He will provide the means necessary to accomplish it!

The unfortunate fact is the problem with people not being baptized does not usually come because of their inability to do it. Rather, it often stems from their unwillingness.

As I close this chapter on baptism, I pray such is not the case with you, dear reader. Do not put it off. If you have never been baptized by immersion in the name of Jesus Christ, do it now. After all, today is the day of salvation (see 2 Corinthians 6:2).

CHAPTER 6

THE GIFT OF THE HOLY GHOST

PART 1: THE PROMISE

Several times in this book, I have called your attention to the three things Jesus told His disciples to preach. Inasmuch as we have only covered two of those (repentance and remission of sins through baptism in Jesus' name), we need to once again examine His words so that we can discuss the third part of this command.

> **Luke 24:46-49**
>
> *And said unto them, Thus it is written, and thus it behoved Christ to suffer, and to rise from the dead the third day:* ⁴⁷*And that repentance and remission of sins should be preached in his name among all nations, beginning at Jerusalem.* ⁴⁸*And ye are witnesses of these things.* ⁴⁹*And, behold, I send the promise of my Father upon you: but tarry ye in the city of Jerusalem, until ye be endued with power from on high.*

According to verse 49, the third aspect of the instructions given to the Apostles was "the promise of [the] Father." Of course, that statement in and of itself, while obviously clear to the Apostles who heard it, provides no definition as to what "the promise" is. Thus, it requires us to once again search the

Scriptures in order to know for certain the exact promise to which Jesus referred.

While there are many promises the Father has made, Luke identifies which promise was to be a part of true Apostolic teaching. The Book of Acts (which was also written by Luke and basically picks up the story where the gospel of Luke leaves off) identifies that promise in the very first chapter.

Acts 1:4-5

And, being assembled together with them, commanded them that they should not depart from Jerusalem, but wait for the promise of the Father, which, saith he, ye have heard of me. ⁵For John truly baptized with water; but ye shall be baptized with the Holy Ghost not many days hence.

Thus, it is abundantly clear that the specific "promise of the Father" to which Jesus referred in Luke 24 was the baptism of the Holy Ghost! Jesus said the thing that ought to follow being "baptized with water" is being "baptized with the Holy Ghost!"

Of course, Jesus was not alone in making this connection. His "forerunner," John the Baptist, taught the same principle.

Matthew 3:11

I indeed baptize you with water unto repentance: but he that cometh after me is mightier than I, whose shoes I am not worthy to bear: he shall baptize you with the Holy Ghost, and with fire:

However, to trace this promise to its roots, we must go to prophecies made long before the New Testament came into existence. While some may not be aware of it, the Old Testament also has a lot to say about this promise.

Ezekiel 36:26-27

A new heart also will I give you, and a new spirit will I put within you: and I will take away the stony heart out of your flesh, and I will give you an heart of flesh. [27]And I will put my spirit within you, and cause you to walk in my statutes, and ye shall keep my judgments, and do them.

God knew that on his own, man was unable to keep the commandments the Lord expected him to keep. Furthermore, God wanted to change mankind so that living as He wanted us to was not a matter of keeping a written list of do's and don'ts. Therefore, He promised to provide man with His Spirit, empowering humanity to walk in God's statutes. In fact, this is what He identified as His "new covenant."

Jeremiah 31:31-33

Behold, the days come, saith the LORD, that I will make a new covenant with the house of Israel, and with the house of Judah: [32]Not according to the covenant that I made with their fathers in the day that I took them by the hand to bring them out of the land of Egypt; which my covenant they brake, although I was an husband unto them, saith the LORD: [33]But this shall be the covenant that I will make with the house of Israel; After those days, saith the LORD, I will put my law in their inward parts, and write it in their hearts; and will be their God, and they shall be my people.

As we pointed out in the chapter on baptism, "Holy Ghost" is not a name – it is a descriptive title. When one considers this title, it should come as no surprise that the purpose of the promise was to provide man with the Spirit which would make him holy!

Although the Greek word used throughout the New

Testament can be translated as "Spirit," the King James translators chose to use the word "Ghost" in most instances where it referred to the Spirit which would indwell the hearts of believers. I believe it was a wise choice inasmuch as it helps us to understand exactly what this Spirit is. In the English language, we recognize a "ghost" as the spirit of one who has departed. That is exactly what the Holy Ghost is – the Spirit of One Who departed. That is why Jesus said He had to go away before the Holy Ghost could come.

> ### John 16:7
> *Nevertheless I tell you the truth; It is expedient for you that I go away: for if I go not away, the Comforter will not come unto you; but if I depart, I will send him unto you.*

A detailed explanation of this concept is much more than I have the time or space to provide here.[34] Suffice it to say for now, however, Jesus was not implying that He had to go to Heaven so a different Person could come back. In fact, He said just the opposite.

> ### John 14:18
> *I will not leave you comfortless: I will come to you.*

When Jesus spoke of the "Comforter" in chapter 16, He was NOT making reference to a Person in the Godhead which was separate from Himself. In fact, He was not making reference to a "person" at all! He was speaking of a Spirit – HIS Spirit. He had already told His disciples in chapter 14 that HE was the One Who would come to comfort them! Therefore, the "Comforter," which IS the "Holy Ghost" (John 14:26), is simply the Spirit of the One who "went away." The Spirit of the Holy One Who departed is

---

[34] If you are interested in studying this in more depth, I recommend you obtain a copy of my book, *Understanding the Godhead.*

called the Holy Ghost.

This Spirit is promised to all. Every believer who believes "as the Scripture hath said" SHOULD receive this experience.

John 7:37-39

In the last day, that great day of the feast, Jesus stood and cried, saying, If any man thirst, let him come unto me, and drink. ³⁸He that believeth on me, as the scripture hath said, out of his belly shall flow rivers of living water. ³⁹(But this spake he of the Spirit, which they that believe on him should receive: for the Holy Ghost was not yet given; because that Jesus was not yet glorified.)

I do not want to be constantly repeating the same things throughout this book. However, it is important that the reader recognize the overriding theme of the message the Apostles were instructed to preach. It should be obvious that, since the Lord's purpose in coming was to "seek and to save that which was lost" (Luke 19:10), the message He gave His followers was intended to fulfill that purpose. Repentance, remission of sins in His name (i.e., water baptism), and the promise of the Father (Luke 24:47-49) are the requirements necessary for a person to be saved. Without these three elements, a person has not obtained salvation.

Just as we have shown in previous chapters that repentance is required and water baptism in Jesus' name is essential, so this third part is just as necessary! Let us look once again at the question Peter and the other Apostles were asked, as well as the response the crowd was given.

Acts 2:37-39

Now when they heard this, they were pricked in their heart, and said unto Peter and to the rest of the Apostles, Men and brethren, what shall we do? ³⁸Then Peter said unto them, Repent, and be

> *baptized every one of you in the name of Jesus*
> *Christ for the remission of sins, and ye shall*
> *receive the gift of the Holy Ghost.* [39]*For the*
> *promise is unto you, and to your children, and to*
> *all that are afar off, even as many as the Lord our*
> *God shall call.*

Although we have made reference to this verse numerous times, there are a couple of things in particular I want to point out. When the multitude asked how to deal with the problem of their sinful condition, repentance and baptism were only part of the response. In fact, they were the prerequisites necessary to accomplish the complete answer. In other words, when they asked, "What shall we do?" Peter's ultimate response was, "Receive the gift of the Holy Ghost." In order to do that, however, they needed to first repent and be baptized.

The reason I call this to your attention is to stress the essentiality of the Holy Ghost. It is NOT an option. Without it, you have not really addressed the issue of your lost condition.

The other thing I want you to notice is that this gift is not just reserved for a select few. The Apostle said the promise is "to all that are afar off, even as many as the Lord our God shall call." There are no exceptions!

Let me remind you how Jesus specifically identified two things when He was asked to explain how a man can be "born again." Therefore, without BOTH of these things, the new birth has not been accomplished.

John 3:3-5

> *Jesus answered and said unto him, Verily,*
> *verily, I say unto thee, Except a man be born*
> *again, he cannot see the kingdom of God.*
> [4]*Nicodemus saith unto him, How can a man be*
> *born when he is old? can he enter the second time*
> *into his mother's womb, and be born?* [5] *Jesus*

answered, Verily, verily, I say unto thee, Except a
man be born of water and of the Spirit, he cannot
enter into the kingdom of God.

The new birth, then, requires both a birth of water (baptism
in Jesus' name) AND a birth of the Spirit (receiving the Holy
Ghost). Inasmuch as this was the Lord's definition of being born
again, we cannot modify it in any way.

There are many churches today which teach the Holy Ghost
resides within a person the moment they believe. Others teach it
happens the moment a believer is baptized. Both of these concepts
are contrary to Scripture, since the Bible clearly gives examples
of those who did both (believing and being baptized), but who had
definitely NOT been filled with the Spirit. We will examine these
examples.

First, let us consider the Samaritans in Acts 8. It is abundantly
clear that, although they had believed AND been baptized, they
received the Holy Ghost as a separate and distinct experience.

Acts 8:12

But when they believed Philip preaching the
things concerning the kingdom of God, and the
name of Jesus Christ, they were baptized, both
men and women.

Acts 8:15-17

Who, when they were come down, prayed for
them, that they might receive the Holy Ghost:
16(For as yet he was fallen upon none of them:
only they were baptized in the name of the Lord
Jesus.) 17Then laid they their hands on them, and
they received the Holy Ghost.

They believed and were baptized in verse 12. However, they
did not receive the Holy Ghost until verse 17.

Another example is found in the conversion of the Ephesian

disciples in Acts 19. We will see that these men ALSO received the Holy Ghost independently from the moment they believed OR the moment they were baptized.

> ### Acts 19:1-2
>
> *And it came to pass, that, while Apollos was at Corinth, Paul having passed through the upper coasts came to Ephesus: and finding certain disciples, [2]He said unto them, Have ye received the Holy Ghost since ye believed? And they said unto him, We have not so much as heard whether there be any Holy Ghost.*

In light of our current discussion, it is interesting to note the question Paul asked in verse 2. It is obvious believing and receiving were two separate experiences. It becomes more obvious when you consider the response of people who believed: "We have not even HEARD about the Holy Ghost!"

Thus, these disciples, who were believers, had obviously not been filled with the Spirit of God. Furthermore, they had been baptized once (see verse 3), AND were about to be baptized AGAIN (this time in Jesus' name). Still, they did NOT have the Holy Ghost.

> ### Acts 19:5-6
>
> *When they heard this, they were baptized in the name of the Lord Jesus. [6]And when Paul had laid his hands upon them, the Holy Ghost came on them; and they spake with tongues, and prophesied.*

Once again we see that, although they were baptized in verse 5, they did not receive the Spirit at that moment. It happened separately.

This fact is further confirmed by a verse to which I referred earlier. Let us consider it once again.

John 7:39

(But this spake he of the Spirit, which they that believe on him should receive: for the Holy Ghost was not yet given; because that Jesus was not yet glorified.)

John said they that believe "SHOULD receive" the Spirit. He did not say they necessarily DO.

Receiving the Holy Ghost ought to be the result of one's belief. In fact, it WILL be, IF you believe "as the Scripture has said."

John 7:38

He that believeth on me, as the scripture hath said, out of his belly shall flow rivers of living water.

PART 2: THE PURPOSE AND POWER

Early in my comments within this chapter, I pointed out how the promise of the coming Spirit carried with it an explicit purpose – to enable the recipient to live a life pleasing to God. This fact is born out in the very title by which this Spirit is identified: the HOLY Ghost. Thus, we are given this glorious gift to enable us to live a holy (i.e., "separated") life.

To explain this, I quoted Matthew 3:11, where John the Baptist said Jesus would "baptize you with the Holy Ghost, and with fire." In describing that accompanying "fire," John went on to tell us what it would do.

Matthew 3:12

Whose fan is in his hand, and he will throughly purge his floor, and gather his wheat into the garner; but he will burn up the chaff with unquenchable fire.

Thus, the "fire" of which John spoke was to serve as a

purifying force. When God fills a person with the Holy Ghost, it is His full intention to remove from that person everything that is displeasing to God.

The writer of the Book of Hebrews offers further insight into this concept of "fire" as he deals with an Old Testament passage. The verses below speak of being able to serve God "acceptably with reverence and fear" as a result of the fire of God.

Hebrews 12:28-29

Wherefore we receiving a kingdom which cannot be moved, let us have grace, whereby we may serve God acceptably with reverence and godly fear: [29]For our God is a consuming fire.

The last sentence is a reference to Deuteronomy 4:24. To understand the writer's purpose for using this verse, we need to go back and read the verse in question.

Deuteronomy 4:24

For the LORD thy God is a consuming fire, even a jealous God.

The reason God is called a "consuming fire" is because of His nature. He is "jealous" of anything with which His followers allow themselves to become enamored that would affect their relationship with Him.

By using this verse, the writer is trying to make something clear to us. He wants us to realize the New Testament believer should have the same reverence and fear of God as the Old Testament "saints." We are serving the very same God who assured us He does not change (Malachi 3:6; Hebrews 13:8)! He has no more toleration for sin now than He did back then. His demand for holiness among His people has not diminished between the old and new covenants. (Compare Leviticus 20:7 and 1 Peter 1:16.)

The difference between then and now is that we now have the

power to live as the Lord expects us to live residing within us. That power is the result of the infilling of the Holy Ghost.

Although very important, separation is not the only purpose behind the baptism of the Spirit. We also know that it is given to empower God's people to reach others with the gospel.

Acts 1:8

But ye shall receive power, after that the Holy Ghost is come upon you: and ye shall be witnesses unto me both in Jerusalem, and in all Judaea, and in Samaria, and unto the uttermost part of the earth.

When the disciples were commanded to stop preaching in Jesus' name, they knew Divine help would be needed. Although they had been threatened by those in authority, they knew they could not be quiet. In order to gain the confidence and strength that would be necessary to get the job done, they recognized it could only come from one source.

Acts 4:31

And when they had prayed, the place was shaken where they were assembled together; and they were all filled with the Holy Ghost, and they spake the word of God with boldness.

There are a number of other reasons why we need to be filled with the Spirit. I will list a few.

*God's Spirit is our Guide into All Truth

John 16:13

Howbeit when he, the Spirit of truth, is come, he will guide you into all truth: for he shall not speak of himself; but whatsoever he shall hear, that shall he speak: and he will shew you things to come.

*God's Spirit is our Teacher, Reminding Us of God's Word

John 14:26

> *But the Comforter, which is the Holy Ghost, whom the Father will send in my name, he shall teach you all things, and bring all things to your remembrance, whatsoever I have said unto you.*

*God's Spirit Converts our Carnal Mind into a Spiritual One

Romans 8:7-9

> *Because the carnal mind is enmity against God: for it is not subject to the law of God, neither indeed can be. ⁸So then they that are in the flesh cannot please God. ⁹But ye are not in the flesh, but in the Spirit, if so be that the Spirit of God dwell in you. Now if any man have not the Spirit of Christ, he is none of his.*

*God's Spirit Imparts to us the Love of God

Romans 5:5

> *And hope maketh not ashamed; because the love of God is shed abroad in our hearts by the Holy Ghost which is given unto us.*

*God's Spirit will Resurrect our Bodies

Romans 8:11

> *But if the Spirit of him that raised up Jesus from the dead dwell in you, he that raised up Christ from the dead shall also quicken your mortal bodies by his Spirit that dwelleth in you.*

I have been asked many times, "MUST I have the Holy Ghost to go to Heaven?" The answer, of course, is, "YES!" Nevertheless, even if that was NOT the case, I would have to agree with whoever it was that said, "I do not even want to go to the grocery store without it!" I do not just NEED the Holy Ghost to be saved – I need it in my daily walk with God!

PART 3: THE PROOF

Having established the essentiality of Spirit baptism, it is imperative that we discuss the Biblical way that receiving the Holy Ghost is identified. Although many claim it is something which only takes place within a person's heart (and, therefore, has no immediate evidence), the Scriptures give a very clear sign to show when a person has received this glorious experience.

Let us go back once more to the discussion Jesus had concerning the new birth, which He explained as being born of water and Spirit. This time, we will continue on a few verses farther than we have in previous discussions of this passage.

John 3:3-8

> *Jesus answered and said unto him, Verily, verily, I say unto thee, Except a man be born again, he cannot see the kingdom of God. 4Nicodemus saith unto him, How can a man be born when he is old? can he enter the second time into his mother's womb, and be born? 5Jesus answered, Verily, verily, I say unto thee, Except a man be born of water and of the Spirit, he cannot enter into the kingdom of God. 6That which is born of the flesh is flesh; and that which is born of the Spirit is spirit. 7Marvel not that I said unto thee, Ye must be born again. 8The wind bloweth where it listeth, and thou hearest the sound thereof, but canst not tell whence it cometh, and whither it goeth: so is every one that is born of the Spirit.*

After defining the new birth, Jesus went on to make a comparison between being born of the Spirit and the wind. As He did, He stated that we may not understand everything about the

Spirit or the wind, but there is one thing they have in common – you will always hear the sound. His very next statement was, "So is EVERYONE that is born of the Spirit." There must, then, be an accompanying sound to *every* birth of the Spirit.

This accompanying sound can perhaps be more readily recognized when you consider the Greek word from which "sound" in John 3:8 is translated. The Greek word is "phone" (pronounced fo-nay), which can also be interpreted as "tone," "noise," "voice," or "language." The wind does not just make a nondescript "sound;" it has a "voice" which speaks a "language" all its own. So it is with EVERY birth of the Spirit.

The Apostle Paul also makes reference to this occurrence, although he presents it using a different metaphor. Rather than comparing the birth of the Spirit to the wind, he compares it to one who has been called to the witness stand for a specific purpose.

Romans 8:16
The Spirit itself beareth witness with our spirit,
that we are the children of God:

The phrase "beareth witness" actually means to provide corroborating evidence, or to testify. According to Paul, when we become the children of God (that is, when we have been "born again"), God's Spirit will testify to the fact that the birth has taken place by providing some form of corroborating evidence!

I have been present for the birth of my three children and nine (at the time of this writing) grandchildren. If I was not in the labor room, I was as close to it as I could get. With every birth, I was, of course, glad to know that the baby was fully formed. I was happy to hear the "ooh's" and "aah's" of those attending the birth. However, there was one thing I desired more than anything else at that moment: I WANTED TO HEAR THE BABY CRY! Only a SOUND could give me the assurance there had been a LIVE birth!

Both Jesus and Paul stated the fact that the new birth would be accompanied by a sound. It becomes crucial for us, therefore, to find out exactly what that sound is.

More than once in this book, I have discussed the "law of first mention." I pointed out that many Bible scholars agree this is a principle that must be considered when trying to interpret the Scriptures. By this, they simply mean the first time a subject is introduced in the Bible, it should be given a more prominent consideration. In other words, the first mention of a subject becomes the standard to which other passages should be compared.

Keeping this in mind, we will go to the "first mention" of someone receiving the Holy Ghost under the New Covenant (which began, as I pointed out in the chapter on baptism, on the Day of Pentecost in Acts 2). Any mention of someone being "filled" with the Holy Ghost prior to Acts 2 was NOT describing the same experience as that which is a part of the new birth. I say this because the Bible clearly states that "the Holy Ghost was not yet given; because that Jesus was not yet glorified" (John 7:39).

Looking at the "first mention" of this experience, we can immediately see that there was, indeed, a sound which accompanied being filled with the Holy Ghost. We can also see it happened in exactly the same way to EVERYONE who received it at that time.

Acts 2:4
And they were all filled with the Holy Ghost, and began to speak with other tongues, as the Spirit gave them utterance.

They were "ALL filled ... and began to speak with ... tongues." This means that all 120 who were gathered there (see Acts 1:15) had the same experience. This did not just happen to the 12 disciples (as some claim). It happened to ALL who were there!

Before going any further in this particular explanation, let me first point out that those who were speaking in tongues (an Old English term for "languages") were doing so "as the Spirit gave them utterance." Another way to say this would be the Spirit provided them with the ability to speak these languages. These were not languages they were taught, nor were they languages they already knew. They were only able to speak them because of a miraculous empowerment which gave them the ability to talk in a language they themselves did not even understand.

Please let me also point out that those who claim it only happened to the 12 are overlooking an important fact concerning what happened among the amazed crowd of onlookers. Acts 2:9-11 lists (by some estimations) around 16 different groups of people who were present, and all of them heard someone speaking in their own language! If only 12 spoke with tongues, how did they speak 16 languages at the same time?

Getting back to the topic at hand, let us draw a conclusion from what we have read. To begin with, this passage describes the first time people were actually "born of the Spirit." Second, both Jesus and Paul stated that this birth would have an accompanying "sound" or "witness." Thus, it should be obvious the evidence the Holy Ghost provides at the time of this birth is that the recipient will speak with other tongues.

Continuing in Acts 2, we see where Peter confirms what I have just stated. He does so by making a very important statement regarding what had just taken place.

Acts 2:33

Therefore being by the right hand of God exalted, and having received of the Father the promise of the Holy Ghost, he hath shed forth this, which ye now see and hear.

This one verse offers proof of a couple of things that have been stated in this chapter. It proves "the promise of the Father" is, in fact, the gift of the Holy Ghost. It also proves this experience is something the crowd was able to both "see" AND "hear!" It was so much more than just an "internal experience." There was obviously an external sign! That sign was speaking in other tongues.

Since Jesus said "everyone that is born of the Spirit" would have an evidential sound, let us see if we can find speaking in tongues to be a consistent proof of Spirit baptism. After all, we certainly want "two or three witnesses" if we are going to establish a true doctrine.

Our second witness (aside from Peter's remarks in Acts 2:33) is found in the story of the Samaritans. This witness, although present, is not as readily recognizable as the first. Nevertheless, it is definitely present.

> ### Acts 8:14-17
> *Now when the Apostles which were at Jerusalem heard that Samaria had received the word of God, they sent unto them Peter and John:* ¹⁵*Who, when they were come down, prayed for them, that they might receive the Holy Ghost:* ¹⁶*(For as yet he was fallen upon none of them: only they were baptized in the name of the Lord Jesus.)* ¹⁷*Then laid they their hands on them, and they received the Holy Ghost.*

Here, we see where the Samaritans received the Holy Ghost. On the surface, we do not read where they spoke in tongues. Although not specifically identified, however, it is unquestionably alluded to in the very next verse.

> ### Acts 8:18
> *And when Simon saw that through laying on of the Apostles' hands the Holy Ghost was given, he offered them money,*

While the Bible does not explicitly state the Samaritans spoke with tongues, it does let us know something miraculous accompanied this birth of the Spirit. This is evidenced by the fact that Simon the Sorcerer SAW the Holy Ghost was given through the laying on of the Apostles' hands. How else could he have SEEN the moment when these people were filled with the Spirit?

Our third witness comes from the example of the first Gentile convert. While the second witness may not have been the strongest, the third one is perhaps our most convincing witness of all!

Acts 10:44-48

While Peter yet spake these words, the Holy Ghost fell on all them which heard the word. ⁴⁵And they of the circumcision which believed were astonished, as many as came with Peter, because that on the Gentiles also was poured out the gift of the Holy Ghost. ⁴⁶For they heard them speak with tongues, and magnify God. Then answered Peter, ⁴⁷Can any man forbid water, that these should not be baptized, which have received the Holy Ghost as well as we? ⁴⁸And he commanded them to be baptized in the name of the Lord. Then prayed they him to tarry certain days.

According to Acts 10:2, Cornelius was "a devout man," he "feared God with all his house," he "gave much alms," and he "prayed to God alway." He had such a relationship with God that the Lord sent an angel to his house to speak with him.

Rather than simply commending Cornelius on his religious practices, the Angel informed Cornelius there was more for him, and he needed to learn about it from the Apostle Peter. (See Acts 10:4-5.) He sent for Peter, who began preaching to him and his household.

While Peter was preaching, the Holy Ghost came suddenly upon them. When that happened, the Bible states very clearly how it was that Peter and those who came with him KNEW it had taken place.

Acts 10:44-47

While Peter yet spake these words, the Holy Ghost fell on all them which heard the word. ⁴⁵And they of the circumcision which believed were astonished, as many as came with Peter, because that on the Gentiles also was poured out the gift of the Holy Ghost. ⁴⁶For they heard them speak with tongues, and magnify God. Then answered Peter, ⁴⁷Can any man forbid water, that these should not be baptized, which have received the Holy Ghost as well as we?

Can it be any clearer than the way it is written in verse 46? The subject of the two preceding verses was how the Gentiles had received the Holy Ghost. Verse 46 opens with the word "for," or "because." It is evident then, the reason Peter and the Jews knew the Gentiles had received this glorious gift was BECAUSE they were speaking in tongues! The "sound" which provided a "witness" of the new birth was heard, and when it came, there was no doubt in anyone's mind as to what had just taken place!

I provide for your consideration one final passage which helps to confirm the fact that speaking with tongues WILL accompany Scriptural believing. Keep in mind how believing "as the Scripture hath said" SHOULD result in receiving the Holy Ghost (John 7:38-39).

Mark 16:16-17

He that believeth and is baptized shall be saved; but he that believeth not shall be damned. ¹⁷And these signs shall follow them that believe; In my name shall they cast out devils; they shall *speak with new tongues;*

In Mark's rendition of what is called "the Great Commission," he lists a number of "signs" that will follow believers. Among them is speaking in tongues.

Some people like to try to point to passages in Acts that tell of people being saved which do NOT mention speaking in tongues, claiming those verses are proof that it does not ALWAYS provide evidence of the infilling of the Spirit. My response is to remind them of the law of first mention: the first time the Bible tells of something happening, it provides greater detail than subsequent records. Those subsequent passages do not have to list the same details. It is simply expected of the reader to know the details did not change!

One example they cite is Paul's conversion. They insist that even though Ananias specifically told Paul (then called Saul) he would "be filled with the Holy Ghost," there is no mention of him speaking in tongues.

Of course, this argument fails on a number of levels. To begin with, the law of first mention provides the basis of our understanding concerning this experience. Second, the absence of a detail in a written record does not prove that detail was not present. Third, while the Bible does not say Paul spoke in tongues at that moment, it is undeniable that he DID speak in tongues.

1 Corinthians 14:18
I thank my God, I speak with tongues more than ye all:

The record is clear. The Scriptures are consistent. Everyone who receives the Holy Ghost WILL speak with other tongues!

The question may arise as to why God would choose speaking in tongues as a sign of the infilling of the Spirit. The first (and most obvious) answer is simply that God is sovereign, and can choose whatever He pleases! He does not have to explain His reasons to us!

Nevertheless, there does seem to be somewhat of an explanation which can be inferred from the Epistle of James.

James 3:4-8

Behold also the ships, which though they be so great, and are driven of fierce winds, yet are they turned about with a very small helm, whithersoever the governor listeth. ⁵Even so the tongue is a little member, and boasteth great things. Behold, how great a matter a little fire kindleth! ⁶And the tongue is a fire, a world of iniquity: so is the tongue among our members, that it defileth the whole body, and setteth on fire the course of nature; and it is set on fire of hell. ⁷For every kind of beasts, and of birds, and of serpents, and of things in the sea, is tamed, and hath been tamed of mankind: ⁸But the tongue can no man tame; it is an unruly evil, full of deadly poison.

While man has the ability to tame beasts and control large vessels, James said no man can control or tame his own tongue. What better way for God to show the recipient—AND the world—that He has taken control of a person's entire life than to control the one thing a person cannot control on his own?

Another important factor that should be noted is that the concept of speaking in tongues did not originate in the New Testament. Rather, Old Testament prophets foretold the occurrence.

Isaiah 59:20-21

And the Redeemer shall come to Zion, and unto them that turn from transgression in Jacob, saith the LORD. ²¹As for me, this is my covenant with

> *them, saith the LORD; My spirit that is upon thee,*
> *and my words which I have put in thy mouth, shall*
> *not depart out of thy mouth, nor out of the mouth*
> *of thy seed, nor out of the mouth of thy seed's*
> *seed, saith the LORD, from henceforth and for*
> *ever.*

In this passage, the Lord promised to make a covenant with those who "turn from transgression." As He described it, He made a connection between His Spirit that would come upon them and His words which He would put in their mouth.

We will return to the prophet Isaiah momentarily. First, I want to turn your attention to a lesser-known prophet, Zephaniah.

Zephaniah 3:9

> *For then will I turn to the people a pure*
> *language, that they may all call upon the name of*
> *the LORD, to serve him with one consent.*

As I've said, one purpose of the Holy Ghost baptism is to empower the believer to live a life pleasing to God. Here, God promised to help His people "serve Him with one consent." That help would come when He gave His people "a pure language."

Is there a language on earth which has no profanity – or has never been used to tell a lie – or contains no words to describe the evil deeds of men? There is none! Obviously, our corrupt tongues cannot be used to call upon the name of the Lord in a pure fashion.

With the infilling of the Spirit, however, comes a new language which is foreign to the believer. He does not know what the words mean and has no idea what he is saying. Therefore, he cannot corrupt the language! While speaking in tongues, a person does not know how to curse, lie, or describe wickedness. The utterances are given by the Holy Ghost. When this is happening, you can rest assured such a language is pure!

Now let us return to the writings of Isaiah. In the following passage, there is a clear connection between his prophesy and an oft-quoted statement made by Jesus centuries later.

Isaiah 28:11-12

For with stammering lips and another tongue will he speak to this people. ¹²To whom he said, This is the rest wherewith ye may cause the weary to rest; and this is the refreshing: yet they would not hear.

When he spoke of "the rest" that would be given to the weary, Isaiah promised it would come with a distinct experience. After mentioning "stammering lips and another tongue," he went on to say, "THIS is the rest!"

It is interesting to compare Isaiah 28:11 with Matthew 11:28. Note how both verses speak of "rest."

Matthew 11:28

Come unto me, all ye that labour and are heavy laden, and I will give you rest.

Kenneth Wuest, in his *Word Studies for the Greek New Testament,* actually translates this verse in a way that provides an even clearer connection to Isaiah 28. He rendered it, "Come here to me, all who are growing weary ... and I alone will ... refresh you with rest."[35] What Jesus promised to the spiritually weary was the gift of the Holy Ghost, which would be accompanied by the evidence of speaking in tongues!

Before closing this chapter, I want to address a common misconception concerning speaking in tongues. Too often, students of the Scriptures want to take every passage that mentions

---

[35] WUEST, K. S. (1973). *Wuest's Word Studies for the Greek New Testament.* .2. Grand Rapids, MI., Wm. B. Eerdmans Publishing Company.

"tongues" and place them all in the same category. The problem is not every application of this experience is the same. Failing to understand this principle has brought much confusion concerning this subject. The following passage is a case in point.

1 Corinthians 12:29-30

Are all Apostles? are all prophets? are all teachers? are all workers of miracles? [30]Have all the gifts of healing? do all speak with tongues? do all interpret?

Many people mistakenly quote these verses to prove that not everyone will speak in tongues when they are filled with the Spirit. To do so, however, is to fail to "rightly divide the word of truth" (see 2 Timothy 2:15).

To begin with, there is a vast difference between speaking in tongues as the evidence of having received the Holy Ghost and what is identified in 1 Corinthians as the gift of tongues. To help make this distinction, we will examine Paul's writings to the church in Corinth.

1 Corinthians 12:7-11

But the manifestation of the Spirit is given to every man to profit withal. [8]For to one is given by the Spirit the word of wisdom; to another the word of knowledge by the same Spirit; [9]To another faith by the same Spirit; to another the gifts of healing by the same Spirit; [10]To another the working of miracles; to another prophecy; to another discerning of spirits; to another divers kinds of tongues; to another the interpretation of tongues: [11]But all these worketh that one and the selfsame Spirit, dividing to every man severally as he will.

Here is a list of the nine gifts of the Spirit. Along with "divers kinds of tongues," we also find the word of wisdom, the word of knowledge, FAITH, gifts of healing, working of miracles, prophecy, discerning of spirits, and interpretation of tongues.

We should readily recognize the fact that there is a difference between the "gift of faith" mentioned in this list and the faith that is necessary for salvation. This is true inasmuch as we know "without faith it is impossible to please" God (Hebrews 11:6). Thus, no man can be saved without faith, yet not every man has the *gift* of faith.

If this is true concerning one gift (faith), it can also be true of another gift (tongues). While not everyone has the *gift* of tongues, everyone *will* speak with tongues when they are born of the Spirit.

When Paul asked the rhetorical question in verse 30 concerning whether "all speak with tongues," he was NOT asking about being filled with the Holy Ghost. He was dealing with the gifts of the Spirit he had identified in verses 8-10. Note that he began verse 30 by referencing "gifts of healing." Furthermore, the very first verse of chapter 12 clearly spells out the topic of the chapter, and it is NOT Spirit baptism!

1 Corinthians 12:1

Now concerning spiritual gifts, brethren, I would not have you ignorant.

Chapters 12-14 of 1 Corinthians are ALL dealing with spiritual gifts that are given to people who already HAVE the Holy Ghost. They have nothing to do with what happens at salvation.

This same fact explains OTHER verses within these three chapters which are also misconstrued. Let us consider two other passages.

1 Corinthians 14:27-28

If any man speak in an unknown tongue, let it be by two, or at the most by three, and that by course; and let one interpret. [28]But if there be no

> *interpreter, let him keep silence in the church;*
> *and let him speak to himself, and to God.*

Again, the topic is the GIFT of tongues, NOT speaking in tongues as the evidence of Spirit baptism. As we have already pointed out, 120 people spoke in tongues at the same time in Acts 2. Had Paul meant for this to be applied to anything OTHER than the gift (which is the same in essence, but different in operation), then he would have been condemning what happened at the birth of the church! Furthermore, Acts 19 tells of Paul himself praying for 12 men who all spoke in tongues. Why did he not tell 10 of them to keep silent? In fact, it does not appear there was an interpreter present, meaning ALL of them should have refrained from speaking in tongues.

It should be clear that the rules set forth in the above passage do NOT apply to people being filled with the Holy Ghost. They only apply to the operation of a spiritual gift.

The other verse which is most commonly used in opposition to the practice of speaking in tongues is found in what is called, "the Love Chapter." Because this chapter comes in the middle of two chapters which are clearly dealing with the gifts of the Spirit, it should be understood that the verses in chapter 13 are no different.

1 Corinthians 13:8

> *Charity never faileth: but whether there be*
> *prophecies, they shall fail; whether there be*
> *tongues, they shall cease; whether there be*
> *knowledge, it shall vanish away.*

I find it interesting that some people take the statement that "tongues shall cease" to refer to a time after the death of the Apostles, or after the completion of the New Testament canon. It is interesting because no such indication is given within the verse – or the chapter – itself!

The verse tells us specifically WHEN "tongues ... shall cease." It will happen at the same time that "prophecies ... shall fail" and "knowledge ... shall vanish away!" That hardly sounds like a description of the "apostolic era" to me!

Furthermore, one only has to keep reading through the next few verses to get an answer. In doing so, you will see an absolutely clear definition of exactly when that time will be.

1 Corinthians 13:9-10

For we know in part, and we prophesy in part. [10]But when that which is perfect is come, then that which is in part shall be done away.

The apostle first describes these spiritual gifts as only being "in part." Then, he states that they will be "done away" *"when that which is perfect is come."*

It is this phrase to which some people point in their declaration that these gifts ended with the canonization of Scripture. They claim "that which is perfect" refers to the Bible. Paul, however, certainly did not intend for that to be what he was referencing. Pay attention to what he said just two verses later.

1 Corinthians 13:12

For now we see through a glass, darkly; but then face to face: now I know in part; but then shall I know even as also I am known.

The word "then" points us back to the word "when" in verse 10. "But THEN [when that which is perfect is come]," he said we will see "face to face," and "THEN shall I know even as also I am known."

It is clear that Paul is NOT speaking of the deaths of the Apostles. Nor is he dealing with the completion of the New Testament. We will see face to face and know as we are known when the Lord Jesus takes us home to be with Him. Perhaps the way the Easy-to-Read Version of the Bible puts the phrase "when that which is perfect is come" will help clarify this point. "But when perfection comes, the things that are not complete will end."[36]

Let me close this section (and this chapter) by pointing out that those who like to refer to verses in 1 Corinthians 12-14 to oppose the practice of speaking in tongues seem to overlook one very important verse found in these chapters. Perhaps they do so because this one verse counters everything else they have tried to accomplish by quoting the others.

1 Corinthians 14:39

Wherefore, brethren, covet to prophesy, and forbid not to speak with tongues.

---

[36] BIBLE LEAGUE INTERNATIONAL, & WORLD BIBLE TRANSLATION CENTER. (2012). *Holy Bible: easy-to-read version.*

CHAPTER 7
ACCEPTING OR BEING ACCEPTED

There are no doubt millions of people today are being taught something contrary to things I have shown in this book. Because of this, I believe I would be doing a great disservice to them if I did not take the time to address a very common ideology being taught concerning salvation.

In preparation for this chapter, I did a cursory search on the internet to see what I could find using the phrase, "How can I be saved?" I went to website after website and repeatedly found references to our need to "accept the Lord as our Personal Savior." A careful study of the Bible, however, will reveal that, although this may be the most popular answer, it is the WRONG answer!

I challenge anyone to find ANY place in the Scripture where ANYONE was EVER told to "accept Christ." No such terminology appears in the Bible. I have asked preachers in many countries to produce just one verse that instructs us to "accept the Lord." Never yet has anyone been successful in doing so.

Let me be clear: There is absolutely NO SCRIPTURAL EVIDENCE which would require US to accept Christ! I find only ONE place that even REMOTELY speaks about "accepting God," and it comes from the book of Job.

Job 13:1-10

Lo, mine eye hath seen all this, mine ear hath heard and understood it. ²What ye know, the same do I know also: I am not inferior unto you. ³Surely I would speak to the Almighty, and I desire to reason with God. ⁴But ye are forgers of lies, ye are all physicians of no value. ⁵Oh that ye would altogether hold your peace! and it should be your wisdom. ⁶Hear now my reasoning, and hearken to the pleadings of my lips. ⁷Will ye speak wickedly for God? and talk deceitfully for him? ⁸Will ye accept his person? will ye contend for God? ⁹Is it good that he should search you out? or as one man mocketh another, do ye so mock him? ¹⁰He will surely reprove you, if ye do secretly accept persons.

In this passage, Job's friends are chided for even thinking it is POSSIBLE to "accept God." Job said that such an insinuation was akin to mocking the Almighty! Think about it: how can WE – humble flesh, the creation – accept HIM – the Omnipotent Creator?

The REAL problem with the idea of US accepting God is not just that it is unscriptural, but rather that it is the exact opposite of what the Scripture actually teaches! According to the Bible, we do not accept Christ – He must accept us!

This is a recurring principle throughout the Bible. In order to prove that, let us first consider what Peter told the household of Cornelius.

Acts 10:34-35

Then Peter opened his mouth, and said, Of a truth I perceive that God is no respecter of persons: [35]*But in every nation he that feareth him, and worketh righteousness, is accepted with him.*

Thus, WE must reach a place where GOD accepts US, not vice-versa! This principle is repeated in the Scriptures.

Romans 12:1

I beseech you therefore, brethren, by the mercies of God, that ye present your bodies a living sacrifice, holy, acceptable unto God, which is your reasonable service.

We are clearly told that living a holy, sacrificial life is what makes us "acceptable unto God." According to the Apostle, this is "reasonable" (or, more literally, "logical").

2 Corinthians 5:9

Wherefore we labour, that, whether present or absent, we may be accepted of him.

Paul told us to "labour that … we may be accepted of Him." In order to find out how to accomplish that goal, we should look again at the verse in Acts we addressed earlier.

Acts 10:35

But in every nation he that feareth him, and worketh righteousness, is accepted with him.

Peter instructed Cornelius (the first Gentile to be saved) that we must first fear God. Then, as a result of that fear, we must "work righteousness."

This is perhaps one of the greatest travesties of the doctrine of "Accepting Christ" – it allows man to bring God into his life regardless of his condition. Instead, the Bible clearly teaches we should change our condition, allowing God to THEN come into our life to help us and save us.

Please understand that I am NOT teaching "salvation by

works" – in fact, I am not even dealing with the question of salvation. Rather, I am telling you how to prepare yourself FOR salvation – you must FIRST be "accepted of Him."

This is not a new concept. We can see this same principle at work in the very beginning.

> ### Genesis 4:3-7
>
> *And in process of time it came to pass, that Cain brought of the fruit of the ground an offering unto the LORD. ⁴And Abel, he also brought of the firstlings of his flock and of the fat thereof. And the LORD had respect unto Abel and to his offering: ⁵But unto Cain and to his offering he had not respect. And Cain was very wroth, and his countenance fell. ⁶And the LORD said unto Cain, Why art thou wroth? and why is thy countenance fallen? ⁷If thou doest well, shalt thou not be accepted? and if thou doest not well, sin lieth at the door. And unto thee shall be his desire, and thou shalt rule over him.*

The Lord told Cain he would be accepted "IF THOU DOEST WELL." That has ALWAYS been the key to obtaining God's acceptance!

It should be further pointed out that there is a reverse side to this principle. NOT doing well has ALWAYS been the key to NOT being accepted by God.

> ### Jeremiah 14:10-12
>
> *Thus saith the LORD unto this people, Thus have they loved to wander, they have not refrained their feet, therefore the LORD doth not accept them; he will now remember their iniquity, and visit their sins. ¹¹Then said the LORD unto me, Pray not for this people for their good. ¹²When*

> *they fast, I will not hear their cry; and when they*
> *offer burnt offering and an oblation, I will not*
> *accept them: but I will consume them by the*
> *sword, and by the famine, and by the pestilence.*

The Bible in Basic English says, "They have been glad to go from the right way."[37] The Contemporary English Version says, "You do not even try to stay close to me."[38] The Good News Bible says, "They love to run away from me, and they will not control themselves."[39]

As a result of their wickedness, God said He would NOT "hear their cry," AND He would NOT "accept them." Obviously, our job is to first find acceptance, and THEN we can be saved!

I have repeatedly stated there is no Scripture which can be accurately used for telling people to accept the Lord. Whenever I have said this in the doctrinal seminars I have taught, someone invariably brings up the same verses to try to prove me wrong.

The most common verses they have quoted are John 1:12 ("as many as received Him, to them gave He power to become the sons of God"), John 3:16 ("whosoever believeth in him should not perish, but have everlasting life"), Romans 10:9 ("if thou shalt confess with thy mouth the Lord Jesus, and shalt believe in thine heart that God hath raised him from the dead, thou shalt be saved"), Acts 2:21 ("whosoever shall call on the name of the Lord shall be saved"), and Revelation 3:20 ("I stand at the door, and knock: if any man hear my voice, and open the door, I will come

---

[37] HOOKE, S. H. (1982). *The Bible in basic English*. Cambridge, Cambridge University Press.

[38] BIBLE SOCIETY NEW ZEALAND. (2015). *Bible: Contemporary English version.*

[39] BRITISH AND FOREIGN BIBLE SOCIETY. (2018). *Good news Bible.*

in to him"). Please note, however, NONE of those Scriptures say anything about "accepting Christ." They talk about believing, receiving, confessing, and opening, but NOT "accepting."

Using the principle of allowing Scripture to interpret Scripture, I will address the five verses I listed as the most common ones I have been given to back up the idea of "accepting Christ."

John 1:12

But as many as received him, to them gave he power to become the sons of God, even to them that believe on his name:

Suffice it to say that "receiving Him" can ONLY be defined as "accepting Him" IF we can prove that definition with other Scriptures. Since that is not possible, there must be something else meant by that term.

In order to let Scripture interpret Scripture, I call your attention to the two key words in this verse. The first one is "received." The second is identified as the result of receiving. It is "power." What we must do now is to find a verse that connects "receiving" with "power." That verse is found in the Book of Acts.

Acts 1:8

But ye shall receive power, after that the Holy Ghost is come upon you: and ye shall be witnesses unto me both in Jerusalem, and in all Judaea, and in Samaria, and unto the uttermost part of the earth.

Here we find the two words for which we were searching. They are linked together in the same way as in John 1:12 – the power that comes is the result of receiving. Here, however, we are told HOW and WHEN that actually takes place. It is NOT when you "accept Christ;" rather, it is when you receive the Holy Ghost!

The next verse in question is John 3:16. While this verse

mentions "believing in Him," we again find ourselves faced with the impossible task of finding verses of scripture which make "believing" a synonym for "accepting."

John 3:16

For God so loved the world, that he gave his only begotten Son, that whosoever believeth in him should not perish, but have everlasting life.

Consider the fact that, in John 3:3-5, Jesus said the unequivocal prerequisite to entering God's kingdom was the new birth. He further explained that the new birth is defined by "being born of water and of the Spirit."

John 3:3-5

Jesus answered and said unto him, Verily, verily, I say unto thee, Except a man be born again, he cannot see the kingdom of God. ⁴Nicodemus saith unto him, How can a man be born when he is old? can he enter the second time into his mother's womb, and be born? ⁵Jesus answered, Verily, verily, I say unto thee, Except a man be born of water and of the Spirit, he cannot enter into the kingdom of God.

We have already thoroughly addressed being "born of water and of the Spirit." However, my question now is this: Why would Jesus say that a man MUST be born of water and Spirit in verse 5, and then, just a few verses later, say the only thing you have to do is believe? Did He contradict Himself? Of course not!

While John 3:16 itself does not offer a definition for the term "believing," there ARE other verses which provide us with that insight. The first one that I would call to your attention is one I have already referenced in a previous chapter. Let us look at it again.

John 17:20

Neither pray I for these alone, but for them also
which shall believe on me through their word;

Here, Jesus connects our belief to the word of the Apostles. Therefore, WHAT we believe MUST be based on what THEY taught.

A second reference that adds clarity to the term "believe" is also found in John's writings. This one, however, is a bit more specific.

John 7:38

He that believeth on me, as the scripture hath
said, out of his belly shall flow rivers of living
water.

In this verse, Jesus said our belief must be based upon what "the Scripture hath said." He also went on to explain that scriptural belief involves receiving the Holy Ghost!

John 7:39

(But this spake he of the Spirit, which they that
believe on him should receive: for the Holy Ghost
was not yet given; because that Jesus was not yet
glorified.)

This is yet another verse that has been explained in greater detail earlier in this book. The important thing to notice right now is "scriptural belief" is NOT equated with mere "acceptance."

The third oft-quoted passage used to support "accepting Christ" is found in Romans. Once again, I find no mention of "accepting." I only find "confessing" and "believing."

Romans 10:9

That if thou shalt confess with thy mouth the
Lord Jesus, and shalt believe in thine heart that
God hath raised him from the dead, thou shalt be

saved.

The problem with trying to use this verse to tell someone how to be saved is the entire Book of Romans was written to people who were ALREADY saved! They did not need instruction on the plan of salvation.

This is proven by Paul's opening statements in this letter. Notice to whom it was addressed.

Romans 1:7

To all that be in Rome, beloved of God, called to be saints: Grace to you and peace from God our Father, and the Lord Jesus Christ.

The Book of Romans was NOT written to sinners. It was written to saints! Therefore, trying to use Romans 10:9 to lead the lost to salvation is impossible for those who want to "rightly divide the word of truth" (2 Timothy 2:15).

Paul was instructing the saints that it is absolutely necessary for them to "confess the Lord" publicly to others. In doing so, he was simply reiterating what Jesus had said while here on Earth.

Matthew 10:32

Whosoever therefore shall confess me before men, him will I confess also before my Father which is in heaven.

The next verse I hear people use to defend this erroneous doctrine can actually be answered in the same way as Romans 10. You have to understand to whom the letter was written before you can interpret it properly.

Revelation 3:20

Behold, I stand at the door, and knock: if any man hear my voice, and open the door, I will come in to him, and will sup with him, and he with me.

How many times have preachers quoted Revelation 3:20 to sinners, using it especially during an altar call to try to appeal to them to "let Christ come into your heart"? However, Christ was NOT knocking on the heart of a sinner in this verse! Once again, look at the intended recipients of this letter.

Revelation 3:14

And unto the angel [i.e., "messenger" or pastor] *of the church of the Laodiceans write; These things saith the Amen, the faithful and true witness, the beginning of the creation of God;*

This letter was addressed to the "messenger" of the church, who was to then deliver the message to the congregation. Jesus was telling a backslidden church He still cared enough for them that, even though they no longer allowed Him in their midst, He was willing to come back if they would only express their desire for Him to do so.

The final verse I want to address will take a little longer to explain than the others. Before getting into it, I do want the reader to be aware that I have produced an entire Bible Study on this one verse alone. Rather than insert the entire contents of that study into this chapter, I will do my best to abbreviate my answer here.

Acts 2:21

And it shall come to pass, that whosoever shall call on the name of the Lord shall be saved.

First, please understand that "calling on the name of the Lord" is NOT simply mentioning His name in prayer. It is much, much more than that.

Matthew 7:21

Not every one that saith unto me, Lord, Lord, shall enter into the kingdom of heaven; but he that doeth the will of my Father which is in heaven.

What I am about to show you (again, in the least amount of time possible) is that TRULY "calling on the name of the Lord" involves a number of things. Each of them are clearly defined in the Scriptures.

Did you pay attention to WHOM the Lord said WOULD enter Heaven? It would be those who do the will of the Father. Thus, calling on the name of the Lord MUST include doing the Father's will.

2 Peter 3:9
The Lord is not slack concerning his promise, as some men count slackness; but is longsuffering to us-ward, not willing that any should perish, but that all should come to repentance.

The Father's will is for everyone to repent. Therefore, repentance is a part of "calling on the name of the Lord."

Acts 22:16
And now why tarriest thou? arise, and be baptized, and wash away thy sins, calling on the name of the Lord.

When giving his personal testimony, Paul said he was commanded to be baptized, "calling on the name of the Lord." Obviously, baptism in Jesus' name is part of this process of salvation.

Zechariah 13:9
And I will bring the third part through the fire, and will refine them as silver is refined, and will try them as gold is tried: they shall call on my name, and I will hear them: I will say, It is my people: and they shall say, The LORD is my God.

Zechariah said that God intends for His people to be refined through fire in order to call on His name. This is further explained by the words of John the Baptist.

Matthew 3:11-12

I indeed baptize you with water unto repentance: but he that cometh after me is mightier than I, whose shoes I am not worthy to bear: he shall baptize you with the Holy Ghost, and with fire: [12]Whose fan is in his hand, and he will throughly purge his floor, and gather his wheat into the garner; but he will burn up the chaff with unquenchable fire.

We see, then, the refining fire is the baptism of the Holy Ghost. Since Zechariah linked that fire to "calling on the name of the Lord," receiving the Spirit must be a part of the process.

Zephaniah 3:9

For then will I turn to the people a pure language, that they may all call upon the name of the LORD, to serve him with one consent.

We dealt with this verse in the chapter on the Holy Ghost, so I do not have to go through a lengthy explanation here. Suffice it to say this "pure language" implies speaking in tongues – the evidence which proves a person has been Spirit-filled!

If we allow Scripture to interpret Scripture, then we can draw no other conclusion that Peter's comment concerning "whosoever shall call on the name of the Lord shall be saved" (Acts 2:21) was referring to repentance, water baptism in Jesus' name, and the gift of the Holy Ghost evidenced by speaking in other tongues (Acts 2:38)!

If you want to be saved, you cannot do it by "accepting Christ." Rather, turn from your ungodly life so you can be accepted by Him. In doing so, it will prepare you to obey the message which Jesus instructed His Apostles to preach – the foundation upon which His church is built! Obedience to that message will result in the salvation of your soul!

CHAPTER 8

CONCLUSION

Throughout this book, I have done my best to show beyond the shadow of a doubt the only way someone can be saved is through obeying the message Jesus delivered to His Apostles. That message was "repentance and remission of sins ... in His name ... and ... the promise of [the] Father" (Luke 24:47-49). Furthermore, I have been diligent in detailing how Peter's message at Pentecost provided us with the full explanation of Jesus' words and, therefore, what it takes for us to be saved.

> ### *Acts 2:38-39*
> *Then Peter said unto them, Repent, and be baptized every one of you in the name of Jesus Christ for the remission of sins, and ye shall receive the gift of the Holy Ghost. [39]For the promise is unto you, and to your children, and to all that are afar off, even as many as the Lord our God shall call.*

Without repentance, baptism in Jesus' name, and the infilling of the Holy Ghost (evidenced by speaking in tongues), a person has not been "born again" (John 3:3-5). This experience – and ONLY this experience – gives us access into the Kingdom of God.

If you are reading this book and have never obeyed Acts 2:38, I ask you: why not obey the Bible and be saved according to the message declared by the Apostles? After all, Paul said if anyone preaches any other gospel than what the Apostles preached, they are to be accursed.

Galatians 1:8

But though we, or an angel from heaven, preach any other gospel unto you than that which we have preached unto you, let him be accursed.

Obedience to the Scripture cannot be overemphasized. In fact, God said He prefers obedience over sacrifice. He also said failure to obey was akin to witchcraft and idolatry!

1 Samuel 15:22-23

And Samuel said, Hath the LORD as great delight in burnt offerings and sacrifices, as in obeying the voice of the LORD? Behold, to obey is better than sacrifice, and to hearken than the fat of rams. [23] For rebellion is as the sin of witchcraft, and stubbornness is as iniquity and idolatry. Because thou hast rejected the word of the LORD, he hath also rejected thee from being king.

Jesus taught that those who genuinely love Him will keep His commandments. Keeping those commandments, then, is not about law – it is about love!

John 14:15

If ye love me, keep my commandments.

John 14:23

Jesus answered and said unto him, If a man love me, he will keep my words: and my Father will love him, and we will come unto him, and make our abode with him.

It is my sincere prayer that this book has been a blessing to those who have taken the time to read it. If you already believed this message prior to reading this book, I pray your faith has been strengthened. If you had questions about (or outright opposition to) the things I have addressed here, I pray your questions have been answered, your opposition has been rectified, and, as a result, you now know the truth which can make your soul free!

John 8:32

And ye shall know the truth, and the truth shall make you free.

BIBLIOGRAPHY

ANNANDALE, C., FUREY, F. T., & BLUMENTHAL, W. H., *The National encyclopedia of reference;* New York, Standard Bookbinding Co.

BAKER, R. A., & LANDERS, J. M., *Summary of Christian History.* B & H Publishing Group.

BARNES, A., MURPHY, J. G., COOK, F. C., PUSEY, E. B., LEUPOLD, H. C., & FREW, R., *Barnes' Notes.* Michigan: Baker.

BIBLE LEAGUE INTERNATIONAL, & WORLD BIBLE TRANSLATION CENTER. *Holy Bible: easy-to-read version.*

BIBLE SOCIETY NEW ZEALAND. *Bible: Contemporary English version.*

BRAM, L. L., *Funk & Wagnalls new encyclopedia.* New York, Funk & Wagnalls.

BRAUER, J. C., & GERRISH, B. A., *The Westminster dictionary of church history.* Pennsylvania, Westminster Press.

BRITISH AND FOREIGN BIBLE SOCIETY. *Good news Bible.*

BROMILEY, G. W., *The International standard Bible encyclopedia.* Michigan, W.B. Eerdmans.

CAIRNS, E. E., *Christianity through the centuries: a history of the Christian church.*

CALVIN, J., & ALLEN, J., *Institutes of the Christian religion.* Pennsylvania, Presbyterian board of Christian education.

CLARKE, A., & EARLE, R., *Adam Clarke's commentary on the Bible.* Michigan, Baker Book House.

DAVIDSON PRESS. *The Holy Bible: International Standard Version : New Testament.* California, Davidson Press.

Encyclopedia Britannica. Chicago, Encyclopedia Britannica, Inc.

EUSEBIUS, LAKE, K., OULTON, J. E. L., & LAWLOR, H. J., *The ecclesiastical history.* Massachusettes, Harvard University Press.

FALWELL, J., HINDSON, E. E., & KROLL, W. M., *Liberty Bible commentary.* Lynchburg, Va, Old-Time Gospel Hour.

HOOKE, S. H., *The Bible in basic English.* Cambridge, Cambridge University Press.

KÜMMEL, W. G., *Theology of the New Testament.* [Place of publication not identified], SCM.

LÉON-DUFOUR, X., *Dictionary of the New Testament.* New York, Harper & Row.

LIGONIER MINISTRIES, *https://www.ligonier.org/blog/what-does-sola-scriptura-mean/*

LUTHER, M., LUTHER, M., HERRMANN, E. H., & ROBINSON, P. W., *The Babylonian captivity of the Church,* 1520.

MILLER, S. M., & MILLER, A. L., *Harper's Bible Dictionary.*

New American Standard Bible: New Testament. Texas, Word for the World.

SAXE, J. G., DARGIN, P., RYAN, D., & GARLAND, M., *Six blind men and the elephant.* Dubbo [N.S.W.], Western Region Country Area Program, Western Readers.

SIEWERT, F. E., *The Amplified Bible.* Grand Rapids, Mich, Zondervan.

SWAGGART, J., *The error of the Jesus only doctrine.* [Baton Rouge, La.], [Jimmy Swaggart Ministries].

The American peoples encyclopedia. New York, Grolier.

The Interpreter's dictionary of the Bible. Suppl., New York, Abingdon Press.

VINE, W. E., KOHLENBERGER, J. R., SWANSON, J. A., & VINE, W. E., *The expanded Vine's expository dictionary of New Testament words.* Minneapolis, Minn, Bethany House Publishers.

WESLEY, J., *Notes on the New Testament.*

WORLD BOOK, INC. *The world book encyclopedia.*

WUEST, K. S., *Wuest's Word Studies for the Greek New Testament.* .2. Grand Rapids, MI., Wm. B. Eerdmans Publishing Company.

ABOUT THE AUTHOR

Pastor Gregory K. Riggen was born in 1960 to (at that time) non-Christian parents, He began attending an Apostolic Pentecostal Church at the age of 11. The following year, He received the Holy Ghost and was baptized in Jesus' name. He subsequently led his entire family to the Lord. He felt a call into the ministry that summer and preached his first message on a Wednesday night at the age of 13.

Pastor Riggen received his Th.B. from Texas Bible College in Houston. With a 4.0 average, he was valedictorian of his graduating class. He entered into full-time ministry immediately upon graduation.

At the age of 24, he accepted his first pastorate. He has pastored in Texas, Colorado, Mississippi, and Kansas.

In 1988, Pastor Riggen published his first book, *The Madness and Method of Modern Music*. He has written numerous articles, as well as several lessons for Word Aflame Publications. He has also written and published two Home Bible Studies.

In 2013, Pastor Riggen was invited to Zimbabwe to address a number of Trinitarian Pentecostal pastors. That meeting resulted in more than 50 pastors and wives being baptized in Jesus' name. As a result, he founded A2Z Missions, which has since gone into the countries of Botswana, Liberia, Malawi, South Africa, Swaziland, and Zambia. To date, nearly 1,000 pastors and wives have received the revelation of the Mighty God in Christ and have been baptized in the name of Jesus because of the teaching they received at his conferences.

Pastor Riggen has pastored the Truth Church in Olathe, Kansas for 23 years. During this time, he has been instrumental in the planting of three "daughter works." His vision is to plant many more churches throughout the greater Kansas City metropolitan area while continuing to oversee the work in Olathe.

He and his wife, Rhonda (Yates) Riggen, have been married 39 years. They have three children and nine grandchildren.

Made in the USA
Las Vegas, NV
18 September 2023

77764866R00095